Learn Computer Science with Swift

Computation Concepts, Programming Paradigms, Data Management, and Modern Component Architectures with Swift and Playgrounds

Jesse Feiler

Apress®

Learn Computer Science with Swift: Computation Concepts, Programming Paradigms, Data Management, and Modern Component Architectures with Swift and Playgrounds

Jesse Feiler
Plattsburgh, New York, USA

ISBN-13 (pbk): 978-1-4842-3065-7   ISBN-13 (electronic): 978-1-4842-3066-4
https://doi.org/10.1007/978-1-4842-3066-4

Library of Congress Control Number: 2017962300

Cover image designed by Freepik

Managing Director: Welmoed Spahr
Editorial Director: Todd Green
Acquisitions Editor: Aaron Black
Development Editor: James Markham
Technical Reviewer: Aaron Crabtree
Coordinating Editor: Jessica Vakili
Copy Editor: Karen Jameson
Compositor: SPi Global
Indexer: SPi Global
Artist: SPi Global

Distributed to the book trade worldwide by Springer Science+Business Media New York, 233 Spring Street, 6th Floor, New York, NY 10013. Phone 1-800-SPRINGER, fax (201) 348-4505, e-mail orders-ny@springer-sbm.com, or visit www.springeronline.com. Apress Media, LLC is a California LLC and the sole member (owner) is Springer Science + Business Media Finance Inc (SSBM Finance Inc). SSBM Finance Inc is a **Delaware** corporation.

For information on translations, please e-mail rights@apress.com, or visit http://www.apress. com/rights-permissions.

Apress titles may be purchased in bulk for academic, corporate, or promotional use. eBook versions and licenses are also available for most titles. For more information, reference our Print and eBook Bulk Sales web page at http://www.apress.com/bulk-sales.

Any source code or other supplementary material referenced by the author in this book is available to readers on GitHub via the book's product page, located at www.apress.com/978-1-4842-3065-7. For more detailed information, please visit http://www.apress.com/source-code.

Printed on acid-free paper

Table of Contents

About the Author

Jesse Feiler is an author and developer focusing on nonprofits and small businesses using innovative tools and technologies. Active in the community, he has served on the boards of Mid-Hudson Library System (including three years as president), Philmont Main Street Committee, Philmont and Plattsburgh Public Libraries, HB Studio and Playwrights Foundation, Plattsburgh Planning Board, Friends of Saranac River Trail, Saranac River Trail Greenway, and Spectra Arts.

His apps include *NP Risk — The Nonprofit Risk App* (with Gail B. Nayowith), *Saranac River Trail, Minutes Machine*, and *Utility Smart*. They are available through Champlain Arts on the App Store at http://bit.ly/ChamplainArts.

His large-scale projects have included contingency planning and support for open market monetary policy and bank supervision operations for the Federal Reserve Bank of New York's Systems Development and Data Processing functions as chief of the Special Projects Staff and the System Components Division; implementation of the Natural Sales Projection Model at Young & Rubicam (the first computer-based new product projection model); development of the Mac client for Prodigy to implement their first web browser; management information systems and interfaces for legal offices, Apple, and The Johnson Company; as well as consulting, writing, and speaking about the Year 2000 problem.

Smaller-scale projects for businesses and nonprofits have included design and development of the first digital version of *Josef Albers's Interaction of Color* (for Josef and Anni Albers Foundation and Yale University Press), database and website development for Archipenko Foundation, along with rescue missions for individuals and organizations who found out about contingency planning when they least expected to learn about it. Together with Curt Gervich, Associate Professor at State University of New York College at Plattsburgh, he created Utility Smart, an app to help people monitor their use of shared natural resources.

Jesse is founder of Friends of Saranac River Trail and of Philmont Main Street Committee. He is heard regularly on The Roundtable from WAMC Public Radio for the Northeast where he discusses the intersection of society and technology. He is a speaker and guest lecturer as well as a teacher and trainer specializing in the business and technology of iOS app development. He also provides consulting services for organizations that need help focusing on their objectives and the means to achieve them with modern technology. He is co-author with Gail B. Nayowith of *The Nonprofit Risk Book* as well as *The Nonprofit Risk App* — NP Risk).

About the Technical Reviewer

A passionate developer and experience enthusiast, **Aaron Crabtree** has been involved in mobile development since the dawn of the mobile device. He has written and provided technical editing for a variety of books on the topic, as well as taken the lead on some very cool, cutting-edge projects over the years. His latest endeavor, building apps for augmented reality devices, has flung him back where he wants to be: as an early adopter in an environment that changes day by day as new innovation hits the market. Hit him up on Twitter where he tweets about all things mobile and AR: @ aaron_crabtree

Introduction

Computer Science is the study of computers and their operations. It includes concepts of computability and how software is designed that are now being taught to students as young as six years old. It also includes complex concepts of the largest, latest, and most advanced computers and systems. This book provides an introduction to people who want to learn the basics for practical reasons: they want to understand the principles of computer science that will help them to become developers (or better developers). The focus is on practical applications of computer science. Along those lines, Swift, the modern language developed originally at Apple, is used for many examples that are shown in Swift playgrounds. You will find practical discussions of issues as varied as debugging techniques and user-interface design that are essential to know in order to build apps today. Note that Swift playgrounds are used to demonstrate a number of computer science concepts, but this is not a book solely about Swift. Not all of the language constructs are demonstrated in the book.

There is one critical piece of advice I give to people who want to learn how to develop apps, and that is to use them. Download and try to use every app that you possibly can. Read reviews of apps. Talk to people about their experiences. Too often, people jump into trying to write apps without knowing what the state of the art (and of the marketplace) is today.

Many people have helped in the development of this book. Carole Jelen of Waterside Productions has once again been instrumental in bringing the book into being. At Apress, Jessica Valiki and Aaron Black have been essential guides and partners in helping to shape the book and its content.

In the course of writing this book, I've been lucky enough to be involved in several app development projects that have provided case studies and examples of the process of app development. Thanks are due particularly to Curt Gervich, Maeve Sherry, and Michael Otton at Center for Earth and Environmental Science at State University of New York College at Plattsburgh as well as Sonal Patel-Dame of Plattsburgh High School.

Downloading Playgrounds for the Book

You can download playgrounds from the book from the author's website at champlainarts.com.

CHAPTER 1

Thinking Computationally

Computer science is the term that applies to the basic principles involved in developing computer software and systems that incorporate that software. It is abstract and theoretical in the sense that it typically is considered outside the syntax and structure of specific computer languages and hardware.

That is the definition that we use in this book. If you explore other books and articles on the Web (including descriptions of computer science courses at all levels and types of education), you will find a wide array of other definitions.

This chapter provides an overview of the topic and focuses on key elements of computer science. This book provides a practical approach to computer science, so you'll see how the elements can fit into your work rather than looking at a theoretical view of computer science. The focus is on how you will use the concepts and principles of computer science in building real apps.

The key elements of computer science are divided into two groups in this book. The first is the pair of concepts that developers use as part of their work every day:

- Recognizing patterns

- Using abstractions

1

© Jesse Feiler 2018
J. Feiler, *Learn Computer Science with Swift*, https://doi.org/10.1007/978-1-4842-3066-4_1

Then you'll see the four tasks that are used in every aspect of software development from the largest system to the smallest component of a tiny system. These tasks are the following:

- Formulating a computational problem

- Modeling the problem or process

- Practicing decomposition

- Validating abstractions

In the remaining chapters, you'll find descriptions of syntax elements and structures, but in this chapter, the focus is on the concepts you use to carry out the basic software development tasks that are over and above syntax and structure.

Computer Science Today

Computer science principles and techniques are implemented in computer hardware and software using various programming languages and devices. Even users get into the picture as they learn to enter data, share it with others, convert data from one format to another (think spreadsheet to email) and a host of other tasks that demonstrate computer science in action.

One of the challenges in teaching and learning computer science is that in order to learn the principles, you have to have enough knowledge and experience of computer hardware and software to understand how they interact with computer science principles.

This has been a tremendous challenge for decades. If you want to learn how to be a builder, you can start by building a doll house or a bird house. Your materials might consist of paper and (if you want a permanent structure) some glue or even staples. The basic principles of home construction can be simply demonstrated and described.

The challenge with computer science is that to build a small project, you may be able to write a single line of code, but, in order for it to run and do something – anything – you need a computer, and it needs an operating system. (This was true going back to the earliest days of computers.) The computer today will consist of electronic components, and the operating system today of even the most minimal computer is incredibly complex. The steps you take to get to a "simple" computer science app are enormous.

Using Swift Playgrounds

If you have an iPad or Mac, you have access to Apple's free Swift Playgrounds tool. Together with the device itself, you have all of the components you need to start to build simple apps with even a single line of code.

Swift Playgrounds provides a massive infrastructure on top of which you can write a few lines of code to start to explore computer science as well as specific languages and techniques. You can run this code in the playground and watch the results. (You can also modify the results and the code as it is running if you want to experiment).

For your own use or for others, you can easily annotate the code. Figure 1-1 shows a playground with annotations. It is running, and you can see the result of the print statements at the bottom of the window. At the right, you see a sidebar that monitors the code as it runs.

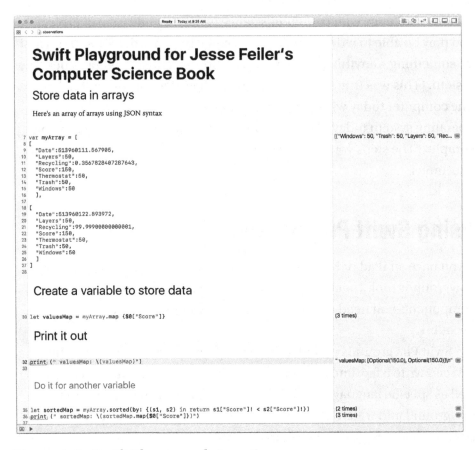

Figure 1-1. *Swift Playgrounds in action*

If you see Figure 1-1 in color, you can see that the elements of code syntax are colored automatically to help you understand what is going on in the code. This coloring and indentation happens automatically as you type.

In this book, you will find a number of examples of computer science principles that are demonstrated with Swift Playgrounds. You can download them as described in the Introduction.

One very important point to know about Swift Playgrounds is that the code you are writing is real. It is real in the sense that it is actual code written in the Swift programming language (the language for most iOS, tvOS, and watchOS apps today as well as a number of macOS apps). You can copy some code from an app you're working on and paste it into a playground so you can experiment with it. (There are some details on how to do this in Chapter 7).

Note   The playground shown in Figure 1-1 is a real-life example of using production code in a playground. This code is part of an app that was not doing exactly what it should. It was isolated into a playground where we could fiddle with the syntax until it worked properly. Once that was done, the revised code was pasted back into the app, and it's now part of Utility Smart that you can download for free in the App Store. If some of the code in Figure 1-1 seems complex, you are right. It was line 35 that caused the confusion. You'll find out about the map function in Chapter 3.

Basic Concepts and Practices of Computer Science Today

These are the basic concepts and practices that developers use in their everyday work whether it is designing complex systems or writing very simple apps. They apply to software that is used for games, for accounting, for managing assets (real estate or digital media), or just about anything else people want their computers to do. If you want details of the history of computer science and the major steps to today's world, you can find a great deal of information on the Web and in your local library. This section is based on actual developers' work.

You can learn these over time as you develop apps, and you can find them in many books and articles. These concepts and practices are not specific to computer science: they are part and parcel of many design and development disciplines. (Don't worry, the following section is devoted specifically to software development).

Both of these concepts and practices stem from a very basic truth: writing code is a complex and expensive process. Not only does the code have to be written, but it also needs to be tested and revised over time. Computer code can have a very long life. (When the Year 2000 problem was addressed in the late 1990s, code from the 1950s and 1960s was found in many production systems. The authors of the code in many cases were retired or deceased, and what documentation that might have existed was lost. Much of the cost of mitigating the Year 2000 problems derived from rewriting existing code).

Because writing code is expensive, it is wise to minimize the amount of code to be written and rewritten and tested. Both of these concepts help to minimize the amount of code to be written. The overall theme is that to write the best code possible (that is, well-written, well-tested, and well-documented code) as quickly as possible, follow one simple rule: Don't Write Code. Failing that, write as little code as possible. And, to put it in a more traditional way, use as much existing code as possible.

Recognizing Patterns

If you recognize patterns, you may be able to reduce the amount of work you have to do by seeing a pattern and realizing that you can implement the pattern itself rather than each particular variation of it from scratch.

A classic example of patterns is shown in Figure 1-2, the west front of Notre Dame in Paris. Your first reaction may be personal (perhaps you have been to Paris) or it may be general – along the lines of how beautiful the facade is. An architect, designer, or software developer might go beyond the personal and the general to notice that this facade consists of three doorways at the street level and two towers at the top level.

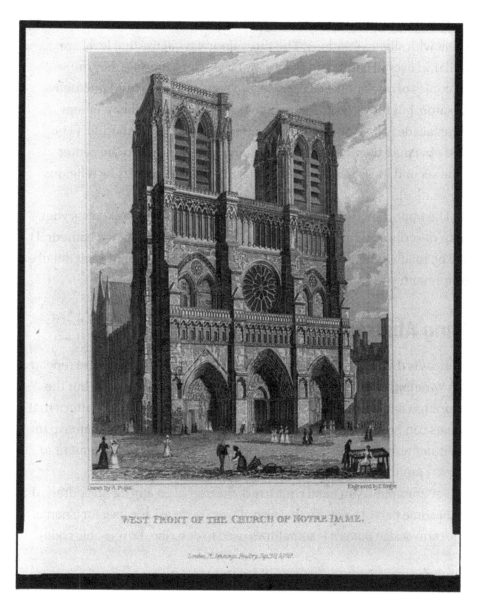

Figure 1-2. *West front of Notre Dame, Paris*

The west front of Notre Dame presents a multitude of patterns that repeat with slight variations. The three doorways at the first level are similar in overall width and height, but if you look closely, they are not copies of one another. Likewise, the two towers are fundamentally the same, but they, too, have variations. Almost every other element of the facade is part of a repeating pattern of one sort or another. (The most obvious exception to this is the large rose window in the center of the second level: it is unique, and its uniqueness reflects its religious importance).

The importance of recognizing patterns is that once you do so, your job in describing or implementing a concept (be it an app or a cathedral) may be made easier. You no longer have to describe or build each detail or component: you can describe the pattern that is replicated.

Using Abstractions

Often, as is the case on the west front of Notre Dame, patterns are repeated with variations. (The dimensions of the doorways are the same but the decoration and meaning of the statues differ.) The part of the pattern that repeats can be considered an abstraction – the essence of the pattern. In computer terms, the abstraction can be what you need to implement to support multiple uses of the pattern.

For example, if you need code to ask the user of an app for an address, that can become part of a pattern that also allows you to ask the user for a name. (The term *design pattern* is sometimes used to describe the reusable code).

Combining Patterns and Abstractions for Development

In practice, developers often work with patterns and abstractions at the same time because they are really two sides of the same coin. In designing an app (or a part of an app), developers look to patterns that they can implement with the same basic code. This reduces the amount of code that needs to be written.

As the design process continues, developers also look for near-patterns. If parts of the project can be modified slightly, a pattern may emerge. This is an iterative, creative, and judgmental process. Frequently, the extreme of pattern-building may make the app more complex for people to use. As a project evolves with input from users and developers, refinements can be made on both sides (user and developer) so that a good balance is made between repetitive patterns and customization for the user.

As part of this process, you frequently find yourself looking at the suggested process to see not only if there is some pattern to reuse but also if there is an abstraction that can be created so that the user sees extreme customization (that is, ease of use) and the developer works on a generic abstraction).

A lot of the coding techniques you'll find in modern software development help you to implement patterns and abstractions.

Fundamental Tasks for Developers

Building on the basic principles of patterns and abstractions, you can actually start to plan your project. There are four basic tasks for developers. Once you're familiar with them, the rest of the book explores specifics of implementation.

- Formulating a computational problem

- Modeling the problem or process

- Practicing decomposition
- Validating abstractions

Formulating a Computational Problem

The first step is formulating your project as a computational problem. This is more than just saying, "Let's build an app." It means deciding not only *what* your goal is but also *why* it is amenable to computation (that is, why computer science comes into play). Computer science isn't the answer to everything: if you want to paint the dining room, it's not going to be of much help.

In theoretical computer science, there are at least five types of computational problems. In deciding whether or not a specific project is amenable to computerization, classic computer science suggests that you find if it falls into one of these categories:

- Choice or decision. Find a yes/no answer to a specific question. Typically, the question is phrased in terms of numbers and values (is person X greater than 21 years of age?, is value x odd or even?)

- Search. In this problem, a body of data is searched and the choice/decision true values are returned. (Of all students enrolled in a school, how many will be eligible to vote in the next election?)

- Count. This variation asks merely how many values would be returned from a search. Note that the operations involved in a search can be more complex than in a count – you don't care who the students are in this case so you don't need to find out names or addresses.

- Optimization. Of all results of a search, which is the best? If the search is for all eligible voters near a specific address, you can use the results to optimize the result to find the voters near a specific address who voted in the last election and have a car (so might be willing to provide a ride to the polling place).

- Function. In effect, this is a search problem (which in turn is built on a choice problem). It is further refined with the optimizable results that can be further narrowed down. A simplified description of a function problem is one that returns a more complicated answer than yes/no or a count. (Remember, this is a simplification.)

If a problem is not one of these five, it is not computational. This may sound bizarre because it's hard to see where something like Pages or Excel or even Swift Playgrounds fits into this list. Never fear: a project can be broken down into computational pieces. In fact, if you really want to delve deeply into the project, you'll find that each line of code can often be considered to consist of a number (often many) of computational pieces.

Recognizing and Describing the Problem

Once you have formulated the problem, your task isn't over. There are still two very important aspects involved in formulating an idea for an app. In fact, these are steps that you take at the beginning and, repeatedly, at many stages through the development process. You may be chomping at the bit wanting to get into code and technology, but you have to start with the idea: what is the purpose of your project? If it's to build an app, what does the app do?

Perhaps the best guidance in formulating what your app does can be found on websites like Kickstarter or any other resource that helps people describe a not-yet-built project. You can answer any number of specific questions, but you must somehow know what your project or app will accomplish.

Many developers are happy to leave the marketing to other people, but you must be able to describe the project in clear and specific terms for many purposes beyond marketing. In the case of an app, one critical step in the development process is getting an icon for the app. Icon design is a very special area of design and graphic arts. Few developers produce final icons (many provide rough sketches for development). You are likely to need to sit with a graphic designer to discuss what the icon will look like. That conversation starts out with the designer's question: what does this app do?

Tip   The conversation between app developer and designer can be particularly useful in the development process because it can clarify the project. This applies to any discussion with a non-developer. Describing the app to a friend or relative can be very productive: they tend to ask basic questions that can help you refine your design.

Defining a Project and Goal

With a computational problem that you want to focus on and a description of the problem in hand, you can move to defining a project and your goal. The project in general is to refine the computational problem at the core of your project and to make sure you can define it in appropriate terms for anyone who needs to know about it (friends, relatives, colleagues, investors, potential users, and the like).

Specifically, you need to start thinking about the scope of your project. Part of computer science is learning to define projects and split them into component parts if necessary. For a specific project, you may want to think about how to break it into manageable components even if you intend to do it in one process. Knowing how to split it apart if necessary can be a helpful backup plan in case you need to do it in the future.

What Isn't a Computational Problem

The most common non-computational problems you run across tend to involve people and data. (Note that this is an entirely subjective point of view based on personal experiences. But it is shared by many developers).

Sometimes an app is envisioned as something almost magical – it will provide the answer to a question posed by the user. If you cannot break down the problem into computational components, you can't answer the question. In thinking and talking about a problem, you may want to pose the question: how will we do this? You don't need to look for an answer in code at this point; rather, you need to know how the problem under discussion can be resolved. If it involves a person's judgment and that judgment cannot be quantified, it's hard to see how it can be computational. If it involves referring to data and the data is not available, you also have a non-computational problem. You may be able to break a judgment down into computational components, but, ultimately, if you are left with judgment that cannot be computed ("gut feeling" is a term some people use for this), you need some tool other than computer science.

Tip   Although not all problems are computational, you can frequently use a computational formulation to crunch numbers and display data so that a judgmental kernel is left. Users can use your app to clear away every computational issue and then use their own judgment on that non-computational kernel.

Modeling the Problem or Process

As soon as you can formulate the problem and the part(s) of the problem that your project encompasses, you can start to model the problem. At this stage you can use any tools that you want to - pencil and paper, smart board, iPad, or anything else. You might want to draw boxes that perform parts of the task you want to build. Don't worry about code - just think about something (whatever it turns out to be) that, for example, computes a person's telephone number (yes, that is a computational problem - a search).

This model might turn out to be how your app is structured, but at this stage, it is just how parts of your app will do things that together make up the entire app. What you want to do at this point is to decide if this collection of tasks or operations (the terms are interchangeable in this context) can produce the results you need. Once you have a rough model, try to break it. What happens if the phone number lookup fails or returns the wrong number? What other components will be impacted?

Don't worry about every loose end in a high-level model, but many people keep a list of these loose ends and assumptions. It's very easy to start assuming that they are all dealt with later on and, without that list of assumptions, you can wind up with an almost-ready app that misses a critical component. (Any developer can recount many examples of this).

Practicing Decomposition

Once you have a conceptual model, it's time to drill down into it: take each component apart and look at its components. (This process is known as *decomposition*.) As you decompose the entire project into smaller and smaller parts, you are often going to be specifying components that will be implemented in code.

As you decompose the model, you may start to realize that this or that component is something that you know how to implement already or that can be implemented using known resources. If you are very lucky, your decomposed project can be implemented with very little additional work.

Rearranging and Recomposing the Project Pieces

But "lucky" doesn't happen very often. In the real world, what developers often find is that if they make some adjustments to the model, the decomposed pieces may become easier to implement. Perhaps the most important point to make about the entire design process is that until it is actually being implemented, everything should be considered changeable.

Take the project apart and put it back together again as you rethink each component. The goal is to make a project that does what you want it to do and to gradually refine the components into manageable and implementable pieces.

There's not a word about code yet. All of the modeling and decomposition is theoretical. Many developers (including the author) think that the longer you work hypothetically, the more robust your implementation will be. Somehow, moving into the code implementation can be a distraction from the design and planning process. Not everyone agrees with this, but many developers do agree.

Validating Abstractions

One of the most important aspects of computer science is that it gives us a way to talk about the development process and about not-yet-built software. Concepts such as decomposition are formalized ways of working in this realm of not-yet-built software. Of course, when a project is actually implemented, the proof of the pudding is revealed: either it works or it doesn't.

There actually is a third possibility: the project description is not clear enough to be able to determine whether or not a specific implementation works or not. If this happens, you can refine your project definition to include the missing information or you can add more components to the project itself.

What you are working with are *abstractions* of the project and its components. In addition to decomposing and recomposing them, also *validate* the abstractions. You can do this by stepping through whatever process a component or group of components or the entire project model will do.

The closer you get to a final project plan, the more specific and concrete your validations should be. At the beginning it's fine to test your model and its abstractions with made-up scenarios and data. As you move on, start seeing if your ideas stand the test of reality. Start pushing the model components to the limits. Don't just use common circumstances: see if your model will handle extreme cases.

If you are working with clients or users, don't rely solely on them. They will be glad to detail the data they want you to work with, but try to get actual data into your hands. You may need to start doing some number crunching and data analysis yourself with a spreadsheet or database tool. As many developers and analysts say, "The data doesn't lie."

Here Comes the Code

If you have followed these steps in thinking through the problem you want to address and the project with which you will address it, you should start to feel comfortable with what lies ahead. Review your problem description to make certain you haven't veered off the track (this happens!). Try to decompose the model you are constructing into components that can be implemented. Check this draft model for completeness, and try to validate it with real data.

You now should have the outline of a project plan using some of the tools and techniques of computer science including modeling, decomposition, abstractions, and validation. Once you have moved into implementation, you'll start to use different tools and techniques:

- Modeling that you can do with paper and pencil will be replaced by implementation using code.

- Decomposition will be replaced by composition as you put implemented components together.

- Abstractions become concrete implementations using real data.

- Validation becomes real-world testing.

This begins with the next chapter.

CHAPTER 2

Writing Code and Using Swift Playgrounds

In Chapter 1, "Thinking Computationally," you see the basic ideas behind computer science and the fundamental tasks involved in creating software - a high-level view. This chapter jumps to the other extreme - writing code which is as low-level and detailed as you can get. The remaining chapters in this book explore specific computer science concepts and techniques - everything between the high- and low-level views.

The Basics of Writing Code

The simplest kind of computer code is the type of code that was used in the 1950s and 1960s. Computers then were mainframe computers and some minicomputers (like the PDP and VAX models). Input was with punched cards and magnetic tape. Output consisted of printed reports as well as punched cards and magnetic tape. (The cards and tape could become input from one program to another).

© Jesse Feiler 2018
J. Feiler, *Learn Computer Science with Swift*, https://doi.org/10.1007/978-1-4842-3066-4_2

Note   This is a very high-level view of code: you'll find more details and more specific terminology later on in this book.

Actions and Data

The essence of a computer program is performing an action with some data. For example, you can write a program to print out (the action) some data.

Creating an Action

Many people wrote a common program, Hello World, as their first program. It was published in *The C Programming Language*[1] by Brian Kernighan and Dennis Ritchie; earlier versions are in other publications, but this is its first major publication. The entire program is shown in Listing 2-1.

Listing 2-1. Hello World

```
#include <stdio.h>

main( )
{
   printf("hello, world\n");
}
```

The text "hello, world" is printed out with the `printf` statement. Everything else in this little program is code that creates and accesses the environment that makes printing possible. The program is a terrific demonstration of the difficulty of teaching and learning coding: in order to do one thing (print out a line of text), you need one line of code and four

---

[1]Kernighan, Brian W.; Ritchie, Dennis M. (1978). The C Programming Language (1st ed.). Englewood Cliffs, NJ: Prentice Hall. ISBN 0-13-110163-3.

lines of overhead. This is the issue that is addressed in Swift Playgrounds (described later in this chapter). With a playground, that overhead is embodied in Swift Playgrounds itself, so you can just write the one line you care about.

Believe it or not, this is a pretty revolutionary feature. (It's not a revolutionary *idea* because people have tried to get this done for years, but Swift Playgrounds may be the first widespread implementation of such a simple coding tool).

In the single line of important code, you see one of the two basic coding ideas: a *command* that will carry out an *action*. In almost every programming language, there are commands you can use to instruct the computer to do something in Hello World.

Using Data

The Hello World program prints out the phrase "hello, world" (ignore the extraneous - for now - \n characters). Programming languages and systems let you store data. If you store data, you can print out whatever the stored data is. You typically store data in a *variable* or in an external medium (external to the program, that is) such as a punched card, magnetic tape, disk drive, or other storage.

Data from external storage can be brought into a program so that what exists on disk or a punched card is moved to a variable inside the program. You can also set a variable to contain specific data. The code for this varies by language, but in general it will look like this:

```
x = "hello, world"
```

x is a *variable*: a storage location where you can put data and from which you can get it back. The data is a quoted string of characters — "hello, world" — the characters and the quotation marks are treated as a single piece of data.

This means that you can write code such as this:

```
printf (x);
```

You can combine the two techniques:

Listing 2-2. *Building a combination of data and action*

```
x = "hello, world"
printf (x)
```

While this may seem like a complication when you just want to print out that phrase, consider what would happen if you wanted to do something more complex than just printing. If there were five separate commands to be carried out, keeping them together so that you can send one variable to the collection of commands is efficient as long as you can combine the five separate commands somehow. You can then send another variable to the same collection of commands.

Combining Actions and Data

You often want to carry out several actions together. In various coding languages, you can combine them into a collection of actions that can be executed as if they were one. The terminology varies by language, but a collection of actions is referred to as a *method, function, procedure, subroutine,* or *block.* (There are variations in the specific meaning of those terms, but they all refer to collections of actions).

You also can create collections of data. In the example shown here, x is a *variable.* At its most basic level, it is a specific storage location that can contain data. Collections of data are *arrays, sets,* and *dictionaries.* (There are other terms as well).

Collections of actions can include data either as single variables or as collections of data. Just as you can enter data values into actions (as in `printf ("hello, world")` or use a variable as in Listing 2-2, you can use a collection of data for the action to act on.

What Happens Behind the Code

The code that you write is designed to be more or less readable by humans. Behind the scenes, there are two other types of code. At the most basic level, there is *machine code*: these are the instructions that are executed by the computer itself (its *central processing unit* or *CPU*). Each type of computer may have its own language for machine code. In practice, today the machine code is specific to the type of chip that is at the heart of the computer. There may be several chips, but they typically use the same machine code so that it can be executed on whatever chip is available at any time. (See "Threads" in Chapter 6, "Building Components.")

Machine language can be turned into *assembly* by the use of a program called an *assembler*. Assembly (or assembly language) is a bit easier for humans to read. The key component here is the assembler program itself that does the conversion from assembly language to machine code. The code is called assembly language or assembler; while the tool that generates it is often called an assembler. The context clarifies whether you are talking about the tool or the code.

Even more human-readable than assembly is a computer programming language. The first languages such as COBOL and FORTRAN in the 1950s are referred to as higher-level programming languages. They are turned into assembly by programs called *compilers*.

Tip   For more information, do research on Grace Hopper and her colleagues.

The hierarchy of programming languages from simple to more complex is this:

- machine code (the most basic);

- assembly;

- higher-level languages such as FORTRAN and COBOL;

- later on languages such as C, Pascal, and now Swift and Python among many others make reading and writing code by and for humans much easier.

Higher-level languages are ideally machine independent so that someone who knows how to write COBOL, FORTRAN, or Swift should be able to have that code compiled into assembler and then assembled into machine language on any computer. Assemblers are usually machine- (or chip-) specific. Thus if you write a program in a higher-level language, it can be compiled into assembler and thence to machine code. Two points are critically important:

- Although higher-level programming languages are *portable* (the common term for running on multiple computer architectures), the compilers that turn them into assembler and machine code are specific to a specific architecture of computer or chip.

- There are often *cross-compilers* that take a higher-level programming language and compile it into assembler for a different computer than the one on which it is running.

Because assembler and machine code are specific to computer and chip architectures as well as the even more important point that most programming and coding today is done in higher-level languages, this book (like most computer science references today) does not go into assembler and machine language except for broad conceptual views such as this section.

In today's coding environment, compiled code is often combined with graphics and many other assets. This process is referred to as *building* (and the result is called a *build*.) The build process is often machine specific. Thus, the code is machine independent if it uses a language such as C, but the build process means that it is not portable. To write code that can run on a specific computer, you need a compiler or cross-compiler that can turn the code into assembler and thence to machine code; you also need a build program to build it for the computer you are targeting (the verb "target" is used to identify the ultimate computer on which your code will run). A build program can even combine several programs in several programming languages if you want.

Compiling and Interpreting Code

Today's computers are much more powerful than those from the early days of programming languages (the 1940s to 1970s). As a result, the very clear pattern of machine code, assembly, and higher-level languages with assemblers and compilers is more complex. Instead of compiling programming language code, in some cases it can be *interpreted*: the higher-level language is processed and turned into executable code so quickly that it happens as quickly as it is typed.

Tip   *Executable code* is the term for code that can actually run on a computer. Sometimes, people refer to executable code as an *executable*.

Using Swift Playgrounds

Swift playgrounds let you write code in the Swift language and have it interpreted as you type it. Apple's Xcode development tool, described in Chapter 12, "Getting into Xcode," combines the relevant compilers and build processors to let you build apps. Playgrounds let you build and explore interpreted code. You can share playgrounds with others, and, as you see when you launch Swift Playgrounds, you start from a variety of featured playgrounds as shown in Figure 2-1. If you don't see this screen, look for a + at the top right to begin browsing playgrounds.

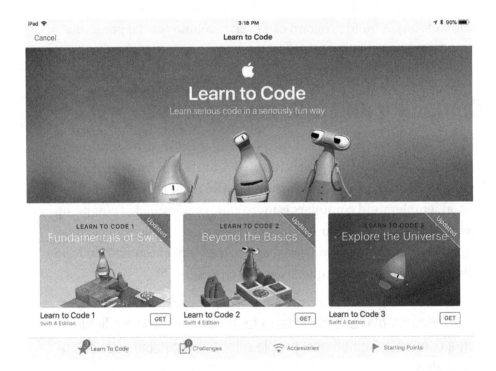

Figure 2-1. *Explore Swift Playgrounds*

Use the tabs at the bottom to explore the built-in Swift playgrounds. Starting Points are good places to start building your own playgrounds. Tap Get to download any of the playgrounds you see in Figure 2-1 or to start working with one as you see in Figure 2-2 by tapping New Playground or +.

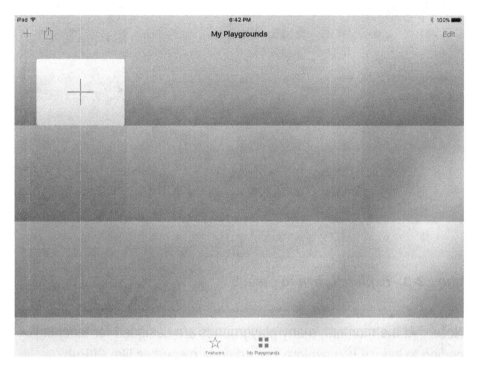

Figure 2-2. *You can create your own playgrounds*

Your playgrounds can be as simple as a line or two of code such as the code shown in Chapter 1. Alternatively, you can create more complex playgrounds that you use to explore syntax and test your code. You can also build playgrounds to share with others. These can be quite sophisticated. One way to get started with Swift Playgrounds is to tap one of the featured playgrounds to explore it. If you tap one of the featured playgrounds, you'll see a description and more information as well as the all-important Get button that lets you download it. Figure 2-3 shows the Get page for Learn to Code 2 one of the early playgrounds.

27

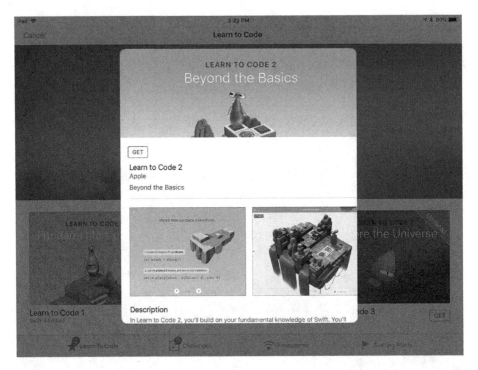

Figure 2-3. *Explore Learn to Code 2*

Note   At the moment, many playgrounds are designed for teaching coding to kids. If you explore shared code resources like GitHub, you'll see that professional developers are using playgrounds for coding snippets, testing, and training users as well as teaching people how to code.

If you tap Starting Points, you can view the choices in Swift Playgrounds as you see in Figure 2-4 (note that the Starting Points change as Swift Playgrounds is enhanced).

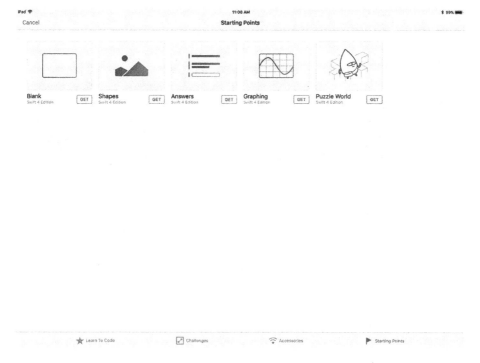

Figure 2-4. *Starting points*

Tap Get to download a starting point such as Shapes. It will download to your playgrounds as you see in Figure 2-5.

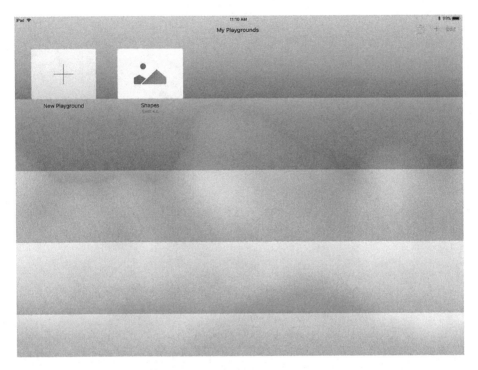

Figure 2-5. *Download the Shapes playground*

Tap the playground to open it as you see in Figure 2-6.

```
let circle = Circle()
circle.draggable = true
```

Figure 2-6.

Run the playground as you see in Figure 2-7.

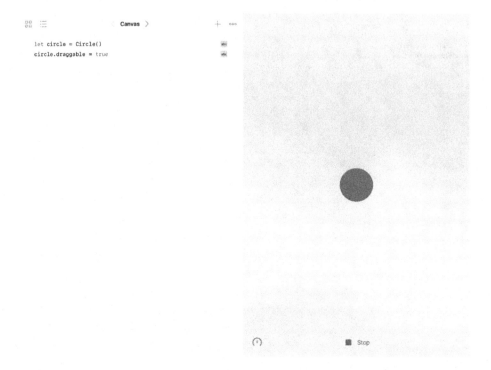

Figure 2-7. *The playground runs*

The blue circle is movable — tap and drag it around as you wish. You've got your first playground running. You can return to your playgrounds at any time with the four squares at the top left of the window.

You can add a new playground to My Playgrounds with + either from the top of the view or the large + on a shelf.

When you have a playground opened, use the three dots (ellipsis) at the top right of the playground to explore additional tools as you see in Figure 2-8.

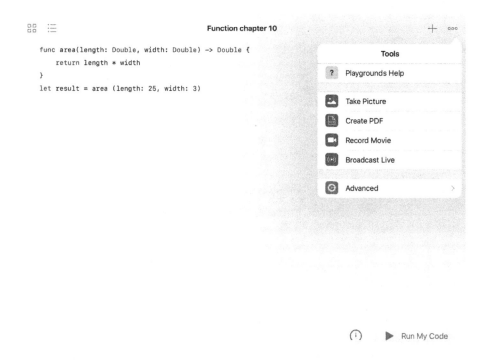

Figure 2-8. *Use More to see other locations for your playground*

In any of the displays of playgrounds such as you see in Figure 2-5, you can tap the Share button in the top right to start sharing. You select a playground, and then you will be able to use the sharing options you see in Figure 2-9.

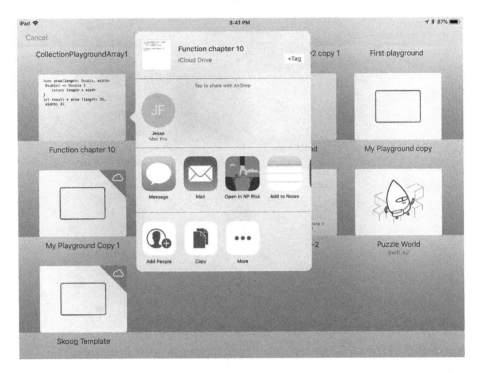

Figure 2-9. *Share your playground*

When you no longer need a playground, you can delete it from your iPad. Tap the list of playgrounds in the top left as you see in Figure 2-10, and tap edit. Select any of the listed playgrounds (there may be more than one) with the dot to the left of the playground name, and then tap Delete.

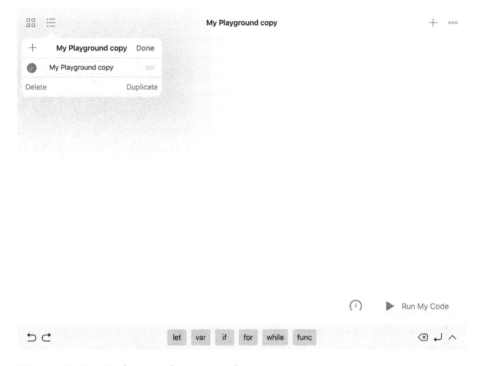

Figure 2-10. *Delete a playground*

Moving On to Paradigms

You now have the basic tools to use Swift Playgrounds to experiment. The following chapter shows you examples of the two most important programming paradigms today with examples of code for each.

CHAPTER 3

Exploring Programming Paradigms

The snippets of code that you have seen in this book so far are just that - snippets. They show a single line of code that does one thing such as set a variable or print out a string. That is the way that programming began: one line of code after another.

Before long, the shortcomings of this line-after-line style of writing code became apparent as programming backlogs grew and programmers found themselves lost in line after line that they and others had written over years. In various ways and various places, developers created standards, styles, and other organizational structures so that the line-after-line style of programming was easier to write, maintain, and understand.

This chapter provides a very high-level view of some of the most common programming paradigms in use today. The paradigms are divided into two groups here. There are paradigms that are implemented in languages (that is, if you use a specific language, its rules require you to conform to a paradigm even if you don't realize it). There also are paradigms that are implemented in the structure of a specific section of code or even an entire app.

© Jesse Feiler 2018
J. Feiler, *Learn Computer Science with Swift*, https://doi.org/10.1007/978-1-4842-3066-4_3

The reason for introducing the paradigms is to show that some of the specific features and idiosyncrasies of different languages are, in fact, common paradigms. In other words, understanding the basic paradigms makes it easier to use languages and code that use those paradigms because there is less to learn that is new.

Note   The paradigms listed here are not exhaustive. There are other paradigms and patterns of writing code, but these lists are the most commonly used today. And all of them apply to Swift.

Structured Programming

Historically, the first major programming paradigm was *structured programming* in the late 1950s with the ALGOL language. From the very earliest days of programming, it was possible to interrupt the line-after-line flow of control in a program by testing some condition with an *if* statement. Depending on the result, the program could go to one specific line of code or another one. Lines of code were numbered, so the control could pass to line number X or line number Y depending on the outcome of the test. Because they were used to control the program's flow, line numbers were important parts of the code itself, and that started to become a problem. In the simplest case, if you wanted to insert a new line between lines 22 and 23, you wound up having to renumber everything, and that meant that a statement transferring control to line 3825 might have to be renumbered to 3826. Line numbering was one of the first problems that structured programming addressed.

Beyond that, a proliferation of *go to* statements (or *if* statements that functioned as *go to* statements) led to a mess of code that quickly became difficult to understand and maintain. The problem is suggested in the common name for the problem: *spaghetti code.*

One way to get rid of spaghetti code and line numbers is to collect one or more lines of code into a *block* that can be identified by name. Thus, instead of writing `goto line 43`, a developer could write `goto computeBalance` or, depending on the language, `perform computeBalance` or `call computeBalance` and the like. This code is much easier to read and maintain.

By the 1970s, structured programming was generally considered to be the preferred way of writing code. However, much old code existed and still exists today, so you should not be surprised to encounter `goto` statements in code that you are reading.

Line numbers are still used in some code, but by now, line numbers are generally considered formatting rather than part of the code. When you use playgrounds with Xcode on macOS, you'll find a line number option to show or hide line numbers in Xcode ➤ Preferences ➤ Text Editing as you see in Figure 3-1.

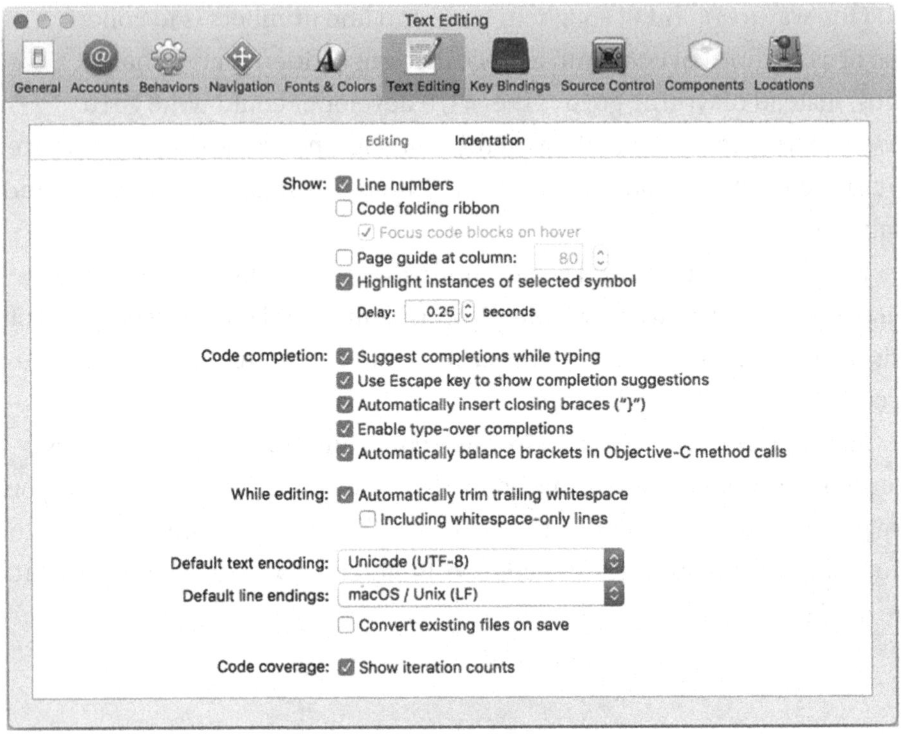

Figure 3-1. *Set line number preferences in Xcode*

Note   Line numbers are so frowned upon today that while you can show or hide them in Xcode, you cannot show then in Swift Playgrounds on iPad. The same playground that can show line numbers on macOS will not show them on your iPad.

Structured program is a style of programming: you can write structured code in most programming languages.

Object-Oriented Programming

Like structured programming, object-oriented programming arose in the late 1950s. The blocks of code that were introduced in languages such as ALGOL were refined to become in essence small programs themselves. A program consists of instructions as well as data. Objects in object-oriented programming are basically the same: instructions and data. The biggest difference is that these objects can be inside an app or program. In OOP (the abbreviation for object-oriented programming), instructions in an object are *methods* and the data consists of *fields*. Methods themselves are structured blocks of code, which, themselves, can contain blocks of various sorts.

Furthermore, objects can inherit. They often represent real-world concepts. For example, you can create an object that represents a building. It can contain data such as an address and, perhaps, the dimensions of the building. It may also contain instructions in the form of methods such as one to calculate the square footage of the building.

Typically, an object is a runtime construct. The code that describes it (that is, the descriptions of the methods and fields) is a *class*. A class is *instantiated* as an actual object at runtime, and that runtime object is referred to as an *instance*. The instance has a memory location. A class can have many instances. For example, there may be thousands of building instances in an app that works with a city.

Classes can *inherit* from one another. A class with its methods and functions can be *subclassed*. The subclass has all of the data and functionality of the base class, but it can add its own data and functionality. Thus a building class might have a subclass of a house or a shop. All instances of house or shop would have dimensions (each instance has its own values for data), but the subclass house might have data indicating the number of bedrooms, and the subclass shop might have data about the type of business conducted there. You can write code that handles a particular instance of building or one of its subclasses either as the *base class* (building) or as the subclass. For instance, you can ask any

41

instance of building or a subclass for its square footage, but you can only ask a show about its type of business.

Figure 3-2 shows the declarations of a Building class and two subclasses (House and Shop) in a playground.

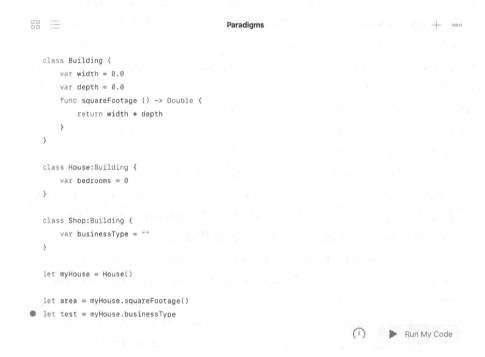

Figure 3-2. *Declaring a class and two subclasses*

You also see the creation of an instance of the House class with this line:

```
let myHouse = House()
```

You can use the squareFootage function of myHouse to set a local variable (area). However, if you attempt to use the function businessType of the House subclass of Building, you'll get an error as you see in Figure 3-2. In fact, in a playground, you'll have trouble typing the bad code. businessType is an attribute of Shop and not of Building.

Remember that as a playground runs, you see the results of individual lines of code in the sidebar at the right of the playground. As you see in Figure 3-3, you can tap any of them to see the value.

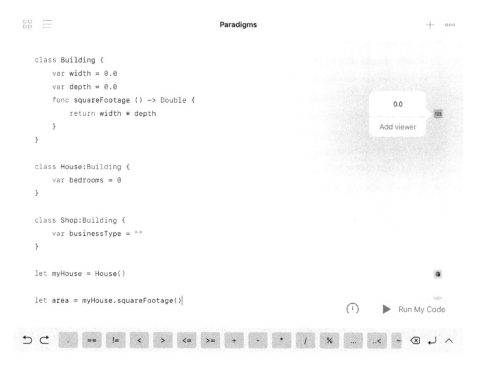

Figure 3-3. *Use a playground viewer*

The buttons at the right of the playground indicate the type of result you will see. In Figure 3-4, the first is a numeric value, as is the last one. The opened result is an object.

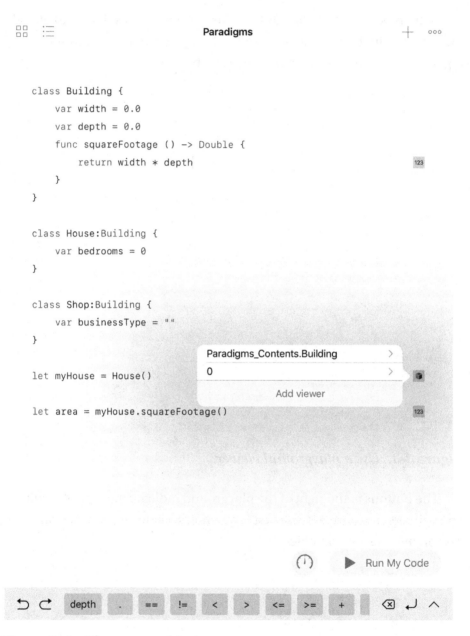

Figure 3-4. *Observe an object*

If you decide to add a viewer to your playground, you'll be able to follow the results without having to tap each time as you see in Figure 3-5.

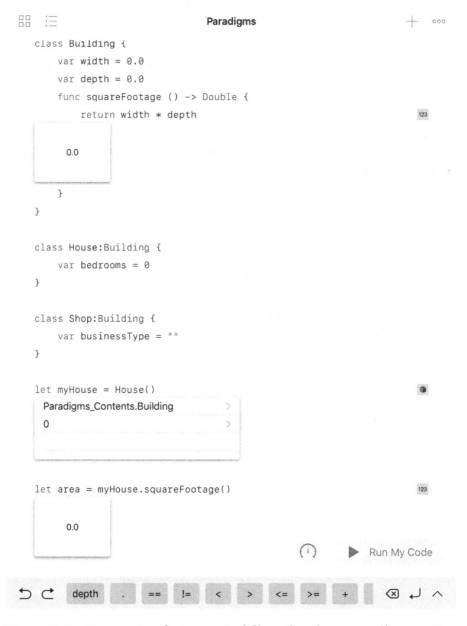

Figure 3-5. *Open several viewers to follow the playground's execution*

This is a high-level overview, but it's important in modern computer science. The most common programming languages in use today are object-oriented. OOP enforced at the language level as opposed to structured programming, which is a style of writing (badly) in almost any programming language. It is hard to write unstructured code in an OOP program, but it can be done as anyone who has been tasked with fixing such a situation can tell you.

Imperative Programming (Procedural Programming)

Imperative programming uses statements to describe what an app or program should do (the terms app and program are used interchangeably in this section). Critically important is that the statements specify *how* the program should achieve the desired results.

Imperative programming today often is based on blocks and procedures: the imperative statements are grouped together into these entities. The statements then invoke the required blocks or procedures as needed to accomplish the program's objectives.

Declarative Programming

By contrast with imperative programming, declarative programming focuses on the results. As a developer, you specify what you want to achieve and it is up to the environment (the operating system and other components) to achieve that result. Certain constructs such as some advanced functions in Swift are declarative. SQL's basic syntax is declarative. (SQL is the most common database language in use today).

COMPARING IMPERATIVE AND DECLARATIVE PROGRAMMING

If you want to find all of the buildings on a certain street in a city, you can do it either imperatively or declaratively. (The following is an overview. For more details, see the descriptions of loops and advanced functions in Chapter 4, "Using Algorithms.")

For the imperative method, you would loop through every building in the city and check to see if it is on the desired street. You would then put these buildings aside into a variable or other storage location.

For the declarative method, you would specify that you want all the buildings on a certain street. The operating system and environment would do whatever is necessary – probably some kind of loop – but you wouldn't be involved. You wouldn't have to write that code.

Concurrent Programming

Concurrent programming and threading allows a program to run on several processors or chips at the same time. In order to do this, it is necessary to impose constraints on how the code is executed because often the available processors are available in different sequences. There is more on concurrency in the section on threads in Chapter 10, "Building Components."

CHAPTER 4

Using Algorithms

Algorithms are one of the key components of computer science, but they go back to days long before computers. In "The Miller's Tale" (1391), Geoffrey Chaucer makes reference to "augrim" stones, which would have been stones used in counting algorithms, but the term and concept go back several centuries even before Chaucer. Simply described, an algorithm is a sequence of actions (usually numeric) that, when performed in a certain order, will produce a specific result.

Such sequences of actions can be written descriptively on paper, but they also can be written in code. In either format - on paper or in code - they can be used and reused in building apps, programs, modules, and other components of computer science.

They are so ubiquitous in computer science and applications that many people don't even notice them, but it's important to understand what they are and how they can be used. That understanding can help you get the most out of specific algorithms and the various techniques for writing and debugging code that are based on algorithms.

Algorithms can be the building blocks of apps and systems. "Can be" because some people would say that data structures are the building blocks, and still others would opt for a variety of other building blocks. In reality, a variety of building blocks come into play for most apps and systems depending on who the developers are and what the system needs to do.

© Jesse Feiler 2018
J. Feiler, *Learn Computer Science with Swift*, https://doi.org/10.1007/978-1-4842-3066-4_4

Algorithms as commonly considered are the sequence of steps referred to at the beginning of this chapter. Note that in that broad definition, nowhere does it state that a specific language is involved: it's just a sequence of steps. That can be coded in any language in most cases.

Considering the Purpose of Algorithms

Why do you create an algorithm? Why don't you just go ahead and write code? The core answer is that an algorithm that is clearly described and defined can be useful in many contexts. The logic and analysis can be reused.

It is expensive to write code. Every step of the process from design and analysis to coding and testing can be expensive. Often, people focus only on the coding part of the task. Experienced developers (and managers!) can attest to the fact that written but untested code is not a finished product.

The first step - design and analysis - is often ignored as people focus on writing code and, sometimes (but essentially), testing it. Design and analysis seems not to be as real as the code and the testing. However, the key to minimizing the costs of coding and testing often lies in the design and analysis. Often a project gets well under way without a clear project definition, and, when the lack of clarity becomes obvious, the project is in trouble.

By formalizing the design and analysis, you create a robust project. The cost of design and analysis can be spread among many projects (either formally or through your own knowledge and experience), but the design and analysis need to be done in a rigorous way so that they can be used and reused in the immediate project and in others.

That is where algorithms come into play. They let you formalize your analysis. Once that is done, you can reuse the analysis with new or existing code, but you don't have to repeat the analysis. As you gain experience in the world of software development, you will come across many algorithms and create many for yourself. By having a rigorous definition of an algorithm, its analysis is more easily reusable.

That is why algorithms are so important in software development: they can help you reuse your work (and that of other people) so that you don't start from scratch each time you start a new project.

Creating a Numerology Algorithm

Bear in mind that algorithms have been around for centuries, and many of them predate digital computers. Many well-known algorithms can be used to find prime numbers, for example. The example that is presented in this chapter addresses a simple issue of *numerology*. Numerology is a belief in a relationship between numbers and events or concepts. Some people think of 7 as a lucky number; others think of 13 as unlucky. There are reasons for these connections, but in many cases it is unclear if the concept of luck (good or bad) preceded or followed the reasons and explanations.

One particular application of numerology is using letters of the alphabet as numbers and adding them up to get a number that represents the name itself. For example, if you let the letter A stand for 1, B for 2, and so forth, the name Dan has a numeric value of 19 as follows:

D = 4

A = 1

N = 14

Total = 19

The resulting number may itself be lucky or unlucky either on its own or depending on the first or last digit (and there are any variations of the interpretation).

Converting the letters to numbers also has many variations. One of the most common makes the numbers run from 1–10 (perhaps because that

51

makes it easier to count on fingers. In the example given here (Dan), the result in a 1–10 variation would be

D = 4

A = 1

N = 4 (count to 10 and then start over with 1)

Total = 9

What you have here is definitely an algorithm, albeit one with variations. It is a sequence of steps:

- start with converting the letters to numbers one way or another;

- add the numbers together.

You can design an app or system based on numerology where one step is "compute the numerology number," and then that step can be done with the algorithm

Looking Carefully at Algorithms

With this simple numerology algorithm, you can look at how it can fit into code you may write. Three basic concepts in computer science are similar to algorithms but with key differences. The algorithm-like concepts are the following:

- Functions

- Objects

- Design patterns

These often use algorithms in their implementations.

Functions

Algorithms can be expressed in natural languages like English or in mathematical terminology. You can characterize them as abstract or conceptual if you want. Comparing them to functions can make both of those concepts clearer.

Briefly put, a function is an implementation of an algorithm in a specific programming language. An algorithm can help you design an app or part of an app, but a function can become part of it.

Objects

Object-oriented programming is generally traced back to the Simula programming language in 1967. Today, it is used in many, if not most, development processes. Briefly described, object-oriented programming uses objects that incorporate data and functionality to be self-contained and functional building blocks for apps.

Algorithms can inform the development of objects, their methods, and data. Usually, they are part of the development process as they are in a full-fledged app. Objects rarely consist only of an algorithm's implementation: that is more often the role of a function.

Design Patterns

Design patterns are sometimes considered alongside functions and algorithms. As commonly used, the term design pattern refers to a *structure* that can be used to implement an algorithm.

One of the key concepts of an algorithm is the steps it defines. Design patterns are a feature of *declarative programming* in which the initial state and desired final state are declared, but the specific steps are not part of the design pattern. This alternative to declarative programming is often called *imperative* programming.

53

Implementing the Numerology Algorithm in Swift

The basic numerology algorithm is described previously in this chapter. In this section, you see one of the ways to convert it into code.

Note   You will see several other approaches to implementing the numerology algorithm (and others) throughout this book.

Basically, the algorithm has two steps:

- Convert each letter of a name (or other string) to a number.

- Add all of the numbers.

The discussion of the algorithm has identified a few open questions that need to be resolved in the implementation. This is common: the algorithm specifies the steps to follow, but it doesn't normally contain code, and it may contain references to external questions and issues that need resolution in order to implement the algorithm.

The most obvious point to consider is whether the conversion to a number is based on the letter's position in the alphabet (1 to 26) in English or if the number uses only the numbers to 10 (perhaps useful if you're counting on your fingers). In the first approach, the letter K would be 11, but in the second, it would be 1.

In order to implement the algorithm, you need to know which choice to make. In implementing this and any other algorithm, it is often a common practice to look at these choices and, to the extent possible, build an implementation that is general so that it can work with any of the choices. The more general an algorithm implementation is, the more likely it is that the implementation can be reused.

The heart of the algorithm has to be the mechanism for converting a letter to a number. In order to set that up, you need to know which numbering scheme to use (1-26 or 1-10). In addition, as soon as you start to think about it, you'll need to consider the letters you will be converting. Characters in software are can be either capital letters or lowercase. When we talk of the letter J, we normally mean J (uppercase) as well as j (lowercase). In converting a letter to a number, we need to know if we will be working with uppercase or lowercase letters.

These are the types of questions that you encounter as you start analyzing an algorithm for the purpose of implementing it. Note that the algorithm, as described in English, doesn't distinguish between upper- and lowercase letters. This type of detail often comes up in the implementation phase.

Tip   Upper- and lowercase letters are distinct. The *styles* of characters (italic, bold, underlined, and so forth) are applied to characters. Each letter and symbol in an alphabet that can be used in an app has a digital value (often called an *ASCII code* in old terminology). This numeric value is different from the numerology value. For example, uppercase A generally has a digital value of 65, while lowercase A is 97. Those numbers are the same no matter what style is applied to the letter.

These questions are general and abstract issues that need to be resolved in order to implement the algorithm. Sometimes, it is possible or even necessary to do such clarifications before any work on implementation is done. In other cases (and frequently with simple algorithms with only a few steps such as this one), you can implement each step separately. You may wind up slightly modifying the natural language description of the algorithm to specify how the output from one step is used in a subsequent step so that you don't have to worry about implementing each step on its own.

With enough people and other resources, you can even implement the steps out of sequence and simultaneously.

Implementing the Number Table

Frequently an algorithm has a step in which one type of data is transformed into another type. In this case, a specific letter of the alphabet needs to be transformed into a number that represents its sequence in the alphabet - possibly using only the numbers 1-10.

There are two common ways of doing such a conversion:

- In some cases, there is a computation that will do the transformation.

- In other cases, you need to look up the transformed value from a table that is stored.

The trade-off here is a common one. Do you store the conversion table before you need it (possibly as part of the app code), or do you calculate it? The trade-off is between runtime processing on an as-needed basis and data storage that is dedicated to the data on a permanent basis.

In this case, the storage approach is easiest. First of all, there isn't a clear calculation that can be used for an as-needed conversion. Beyond that, the amount of data to be stored is so small that you won't have difficulty storing it even on the smallest device.

Having decided to store the data, the question for the implementation is How? Swift can interact with a variety of databases, but, like most programming languages, it has a variety of language elements that are used to store and manage data. These include sets, arrays, and dictionaries, which are described more fully in Chapter 6, "Working with Data: Collections." This implementation of numerology numbers will serve as an introduction to Swift dictionaries, the mechanism used in this implementation.

A Swift dictionary is an *associative array*. Arrays themselves are collections of ordered data such as the name of each student in a class. Each item (student) in the collection is identified by a number. This allows you to access the appropriate item as you need to. It also lets you loop through all of the items by referring to their numbers (they are called *index numbers* or *indexes*). If you delete an item from an array, the other items are moved up. In other words, if you delete item 8, item 9 becomes item 8. The index numbers vary over time for each specific item.

An associative array doesn't use index numbers: Instead, it uses a *key* - often a string - to identify each item. Thus, if you use the string "eight" to identify an item in an associative array, that is and will remain the key for that item. In an array the items might be numbered 7, 8, 9, and if you delete item 8 you will have 7 and 8 because 8 is deleted and 9 becomes 8. In an associative array, if your keys are "seven," "eight," and "nine," and you delete "eight," you will have "seven" and "nine." (In other languages, associative arrays may be called hashes, hash tables, or maps.)

Tip   This a trade-off between storage and processing. You will find some old documentation and practitioners who argue that the cost of the computation to look up each key at runtime slows down the app. Logically it does, but with today's processors, that "delay" is unlikely to be meaningful. Write for today's devices!

Swift dictionaries consist of pairs of keys and values. The keys can be any type, but often are strings. The values can be any type that conforms to the Hashable protocol. (This is described in Chapter 6.) The value can be any type that you choose, but it must be same for all entries in the dictionary. However, you can use types such as AnyObject for the values, which give you a lot of leeway.

You can begin by declaring a variable of numerology numbers for each letter of the alphabet. Listing 4-1 shows what that might look like. In a declaration of a dictionary in Swift, the key/value pairs are shown separated by a colon. The entire list is enclosed in square brackets. (Note that, as you see in Chapter 6, you can add or delete dictionary entries.)

Listing 4-1. Numerology dictionary

```
let numbers = [
  "a" : 1,
  "b" : 2,
  "c" : 3,
  "d" : 4,
  "e" : 5,
  "f" : 6,
  "g" : 7,
  "h" : 8,
  "i" : 9,
  "j" : 10,
  "k" : 11,
  "l" : 12,
  "m" : 13,
  "n" : 14,
  "o" : 15,
  "p" : 16,
  "q" : 17,
  "r" : 18,
  "s" : 19,
  "t" : 20,
  "u" : 21,
  "v" : 22,
```

```
  "w" : 23,
  "x" : 24,
  "y" : 25,
  "z" : 26
]
```

To access the value for a specific key, you can use code such as this:

```
numbers["y"]
```

In an array, each index has a data element (you cannot access an index beyond the bounds of the array, but otherwise you can access any element). In a dictionary, the keys do not change as you add or delete data. This means that the key "y" might have no value associated with it. Therefore, when you access a key in a dictionary, Swift returns an optional value that might be null. You can test to see if it is null, or you can unwrap it with ? or !. (Find out more in the section, "Handling Data That Isn't There (Optionals)," in Chapter 7.)

The dictionary structure can help you answer the question of upper- and lowercase letters. Although keys must be unique, values do not need to be. Thus, you can create a dictionary with both upper- and lowercase letters for keys as you see in Listing 4-2.

Listing 4-2. Add uppercase letters

```
let numbers = [
  "a" : 1,
  "A" : 1,
  "b" : 2,
  "B" : 2,
  "c" : 3,
  "C" : 3,
  "d" : 4,
  "D" : 4,
```

```
"e" : 5,
"E" : 5,
"f" : 6,
"F" : 6,
"g" : 7,
"G" : 7,
"h" : 8,
"H" : 8,
"i" : 9,
"I" : 9,
"j" : 10,
"J" : 10,
"k" : 11,
"K" : 11,
"l" : 12,
"L" : 12,
"m" : 13,
"M" : 13,
"n" : 14,
"N" : 14,
"o" : 15,
"O" : 15,
"p" : 16,
"P" : 16,
"q" : 17,
"Q" : 17,
"r" : 18,
"R" : 18,
"s" : 19,
"S" : 19,
"t" : 20,
"T" : 20,
```

```
      "u" : 21,
      "U" : 21,
      "v" : 22,
      "V" : 22,
      "w" : 23,
      "W" : 23,
      "x" : 24,
      "X" : 24,
      "y" : 25,
      "Y" : 25,
      "z" : 26,
      "Z" : 26
]
```

If you want to unwrap the element, you can use code such as this:

```
print ("j force unwrapped: ", numbers["j"]!)
```

If you want to use a better and safer method, use the conditional cast operator (as?) as you see here:

```
if let myValue = numbers ["r"] as? Int {
  print ("myValue = ", myValue)
} else {
  print ("no value")
}
```

The results are shown in Figure 4-1.

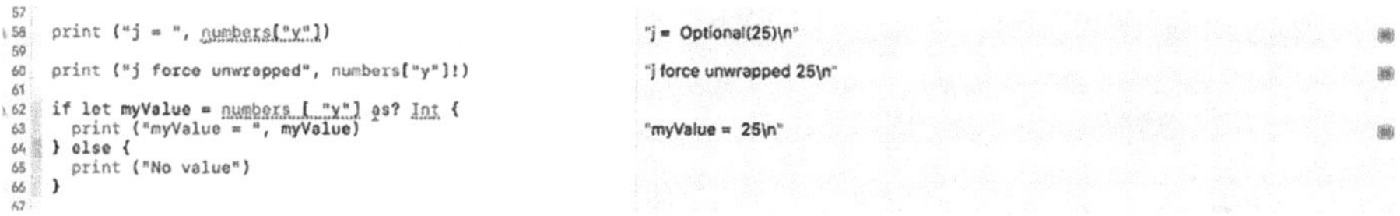

Figure 4-1. *Testing the dictionary*

Note in the sidebar that the Swift playground distinguishes between optionals, forced unwrapped values, and values themselves.

Implementing the Addition

The addition process requires two steps:

- Split the name into individual characters.

- Look up the numeric value of each one.

These two steps are inside a loop - you might want to call the loop itself a step with two substeps.

You can set a variable to a name, then split it apart into individual characters.

Here is the code to use if you want to use Swift's string subscript syntax:

```
let name = "Jesse"
for character in "name" {
print character
}
```

You need to be able to convert a character to its appropriate value. Although the keys in a dictionary are unique, the values are not. Thus, the code that you use to convert a value to a key is an optional (it may be nil if there is no value for the key), and it may be an array (if there is more than one value for the key).

The code to look up the keys for a value is shown in Figure 4-2.

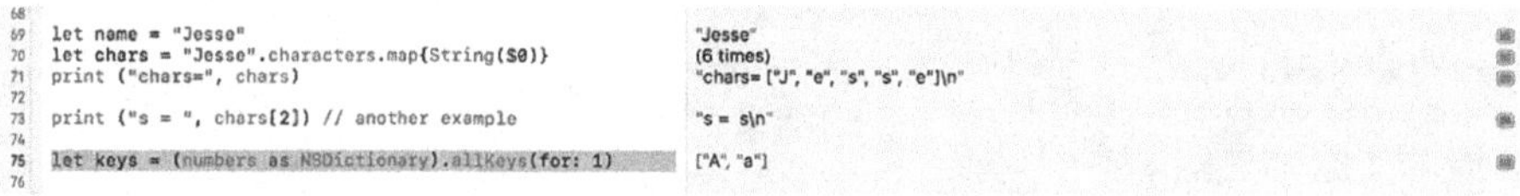

```
68
69  let name = "Jesse"                                  "Jesse"
70  let chars = "Jesse".characters.map{String($0)}      (6 times)
71  print ("chars=", chars)                             "chars= ["J", "e", "s", "s", "e"]\n"
72
73  print ("s = ", chars[2]) // another example         "s = s\n"
74
75  let keys = (numbers as NSDictionary).allKeys(for: 1) ["A", "a"]
76
```

Figure 4-2. *Look up a key for a value*

If you want to use the Swift 4 String map function, you can separate each character using a closure that takes advantage of the fact that a Swift 4 String is a collection of characters. The code is shown here:

```
let name = "Jesse"
let x = name.map {Character in
  print (Character)
}
```

This code merely disassembles and reassembles the characters and string, but it is the beginning of the code you will need in the next step.

Now that you have seen how to split the string into characters, you can loop through each character in turn. Listing 4-3 shows the code to loop through each character.

Listing 4-3. Loop through each key

```
if keys.count > 0 {
  print ("Keys for 1: ", keys)
} else {
  "No Key for value"
}
```

Note that it is prudent to check that there is at least one key to look up. You can experiment with these lines of code to go through all of the elements in the dictionary.

You should be comfortable with manipulating the dictionary, so it's time to look up the values for each letter and add them up. Listing 4-4 shows that loop along with the initialization of the total variable that will be used to accumulate the values.

Listing 4-4. Adding up the looked-up numbers

```
var total = 0
for eachKey in chars {
  if let key = numbers[eachKey] {
    print ("Looked-up key value for ", eachKey,
numbers[eachKey]!)
    total += numbers[eachKey]!
  }
}

print ("Total: ", total)
```

Figure 4-3 shows the playground and the output (the top part is not shown because it is repetitive).

Figure 4-3. *Running the app in a playground*

There's one more point to observe before moving on. If you look at the top of the playground as shown in Figure 4-4, you'll see that the items in a dictionary are in no order. Arrays are ordered, but dictionaries are not.

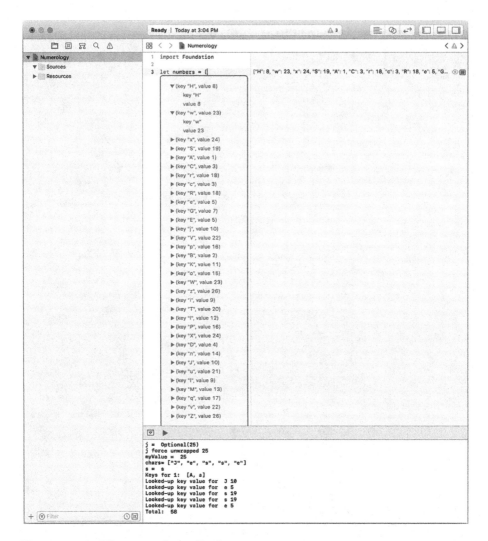

Figure 4-4. *Elements in a dictionary*

If you want to see how to duplicate Figure 4-4, repeat the code. Then tap the Show Result button at the right of the first line of code. That will open the result view at the left. Drag the bottom of the frame down to enlarge the result to show as much of the let statement as you want to see. You can open or close the disclosure triangles to see the data.

Summary

This chapter shows you the basics of algorithms - ordered steps to perform an operation. They can be described in English or mathematically, but they come to life when implemented in a specific language.

CHAPTER 5

Managing Control Flow: Repetition

Algorithms consist of steps to take to solve a problem, compute a result, or otherwise do the work of an app or part of it. Each step is normally executed in turn, and, at the end of the process, your work is done.

This type of programming has a name: it is *procedural* or *imperative* (those words are used in their normal common meanings). (The word for a type of programming such as this is a *paradigm* so you will see references to the imperative paradigm in many places).

The contrasting paradigm is *declarative* or *functional* programming. The two paradigms coexist often in the same app or program. Both have their roots in the earliest days of computers and computer programming, but in a vast overgeneralization, it is possible to say that declarative/ functional programming had its roots in mathematics and logic while procedural/imperative programming was the paradigm of choice among the engineers who built the first computers.

Both paradigms are useful, and, because of that as well as the fact that you may find both in the same project, we take no sides in the occasional argument as to which is better. They're both necessary and useful is this book's mantra.

© Jesse Feiler 2018
J. Feiler, *Learn Computer Science with Swift*, https://doi.org/10.1007/978-1-4842-3066-4_5

Getting Ready for a Multi-Step Control Flow Project with Random Numbers

To explore a multi-step project and its control, you need something to work with. One of the most common uses of multi-step projects is in managing collections of data such as arrays. (There is more on arrays in Chapter 6, Structuring Data - The Swift Issues.)

An array is like a list — a list of students in a classroom, items on a shopping list, stops on an itinerary — any list at all. The simplest list to work with is a list of numbers. Numbers carry almost no meaning, so you won't be distracted by a list that might place Paris between Melbourne and Auckland.

In order to have a set of numbers that really is meaningless, computer scientists often use *random numbers*. Random numbers are just that — numbers picked at random. Random numbers are used in many practical applications. For example, if you have bowl full of raffle tickets, you often would pick one *at random* to choose a winner of the raffle.

Random numbers are used in a variety of computer science processes from automatically choosing game pieces and situations in a game to statistical sampling and the conduct of randomized testing of drugs and treatments as well as other scientific experiments. Because random numbers are used in so many ways (including demonstrating computer science control structures as in this chapter), it is useful to look at how you create them for any of these purposes.

The first point to consider is that truly random numbers are hard to create. In practice, they are usually generated by a series of calculations that are designed to eliminate any patterns and therefore can be considered to be random numbers. For this reason, the term *pseudo-random numbers* is often used by people who want to be precise. For the purposes of this book (and many other common purposes), the pseudo-random numbers are fine for use; in this section, we use *random number* in its broadest sense.

Swift and playgrounds provide three built-in functions to produce random numbers. They produce random numbers that you can then use for your own purposes. You do not need to refer to a list of random numbers (such lists do exist). They provide you with a random number that is either between 0 and 1 or between 0 and an upper limit that you provide. These numbers are returned as integers (specifically UInt32) or a double in the case of `drand48()`.

The three built-in Swift functions that generate random numbers are as follows:

> `arc4random_uniform(_:)` takes a single parameter which must be an integer.

The random number will be between 0 and the parameter minus 1. Thus, a call to arc4random_uniform(10) will return a value between 0 and 9.

`drand48()` returns a random number of double type. You do not specify the range: the number will fall between 0 and 1.

`arc4random()` takes no parameters. The resulting number will be between 0 and 2 ** 32-1.

In the case of `drand48`, you can take the resulting number and multiply it by any value you want in order to get a random number between 0 and that number. With `arc4random_uniform(_:)` you just provide the upper bound so no multiplication is required.

Note that when you convert numbers from one type to another (float or double to or from one of the integer types), the conversion process may introduce some non-random aspects to the resulting number. For almost all common purposes, this doesn't matter.

If you want to preserve the randomness of the returned number, avoid too much type conversion and manipulation. Particularly with floating-point numbers, those calculations can introduce some non-random elements into the mix. However, as pointed out previously, this is usually not a problem in most applications of random numbers.

Creating a Random Number Playground

You can build on the Answers playground that is distributed with iOS so that you can experiment with random numbers. Here is a way to do that. With the shelf showing, tap + at the top right, and then tap the New Playground + button as you see in Figure 5-1.

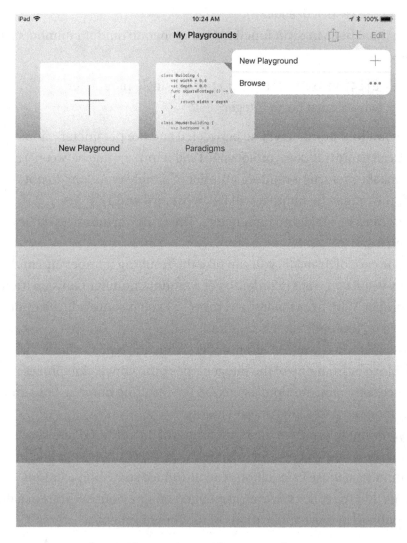

Figure 5-1. *Duplicate the Answers playground*

Tap the Starting Points tab at the bottom as shown in Figure 5-2 and then get Answers by tapping its Get button.

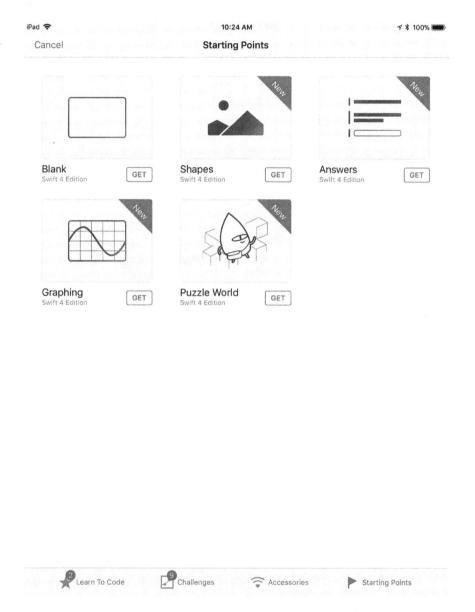

Figure 5-2. *Get Answers*

A copy of Answers will be created for you as you see in Figure 5-3.

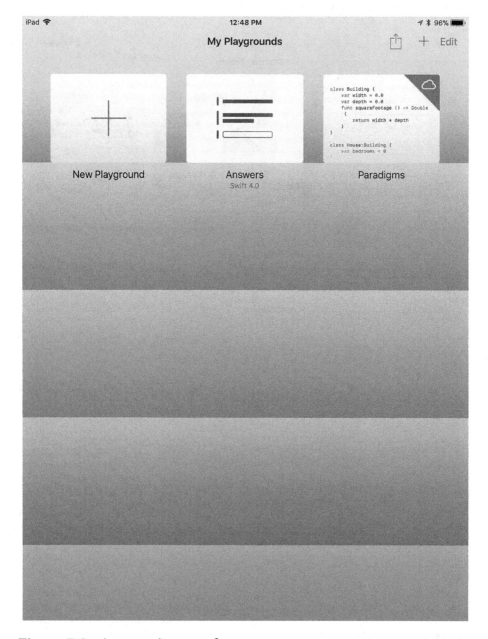

Figure 5-3. *Answers is created*

Tap Answers to open it as you see in Figure 5-4.

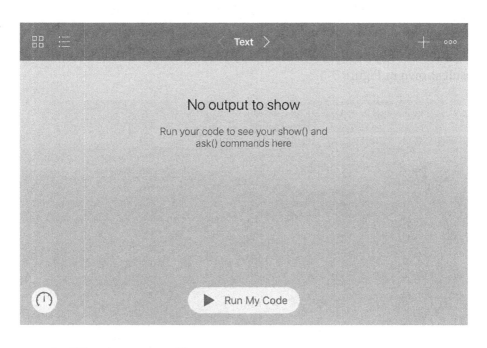

```
show("What is your name?")

let name = ask("Name")

show("Hi " + name)
```

Figure 5-4. *Open Answers*

When you download a playground (or a template in Xcode), the safest thing to do is to see if it runs as-is. Not all templates and playgrounds are configured to run, but it's a good idea to see if you do have a running playground. Tap the playground's Run My Code button. You'll see the result shown in Figure 5-5.

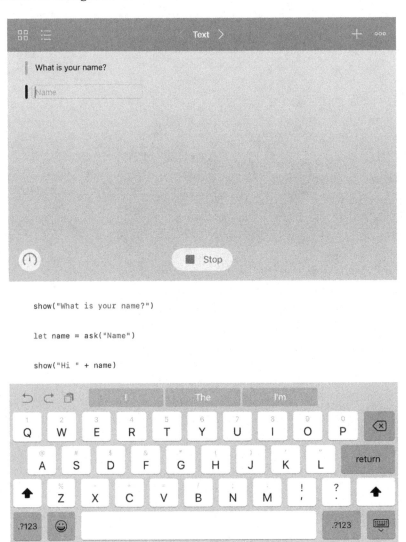

```
show("What is your name?")

let name = ask("Name")

show("Hi " + name)
```

Figure 5-5. *Run Answers*

At the top of the playground, you see its result — a prompt and a data entry field. Below that is a Stop button. Then you find the code itself and the keyboard.

What you've got now in the Answers playground is an interactive playground that displays a prompt and lets people enter a response. You're ready to build on that.

Writing the Playground Code

You can build on existing code in Answers to ask people to enter an upper limit for a random number to be generated using arc4random_uniiform(_:) - the function that returns a pseudo-random number between 0 and the upper limit given (minus 1 so the upper limit is outside the range of random numbers). The result is a UInt32.

Here is the modified code.

First, ask the user to enter the upper limit:

```
show ("What is your name?")
becomes
show ("Upper limit for random number?")

let name = ask ("Name")
becomes
let upperLimit = ask ("Upper Limit")

show ("Hi " + name)
becomes
show (upperLimit)
```

You've now got a playground that runs and asks for a random number limit and then shows the result. You can use the Swift playground to modify the code. As you proceed, the shortcut bar and prompts will help you write your code.

The input data is a string, so you'll need to convert it to an integer with this code:

```
let intResponse = UInt32(upperLimit)
```

Generate the random number:

```
let random = arc4random_uniform(intResponse!)
```

random will be an integer, so convert it to a string for display

```
let randomString = String(random)
```

Finally show the result.

```
show (randomString)
```

Figure 5-6 shows the playground running. The upper limit is entered as 49 and the random number generated is 25.

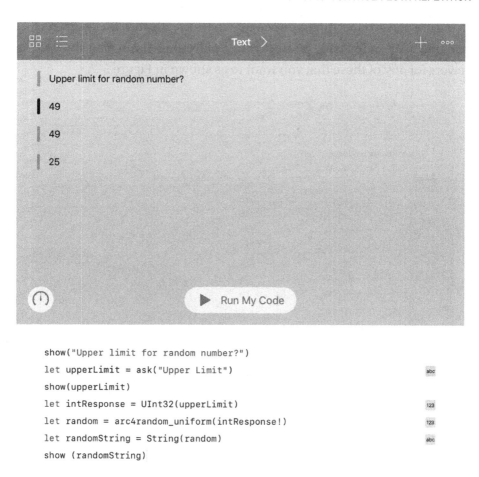

```
show("Upper limit for random number?")
let upperLimit = ask("Upper Limit")                      abc
show(upperLimit)
let intResponse = UInt32(upperLimit)                     123
let random = arc4random_uniform(intResponse!)            123
let randomString = String(random)                        abc
show (randomString)
```

Figure 5-6. *Start to run the new playground*

As the playground runs, you see that there are displayable results for each line of executed code (as always in a playground). You can show viewers for any of these that you want to as shown in Figure 5-7.

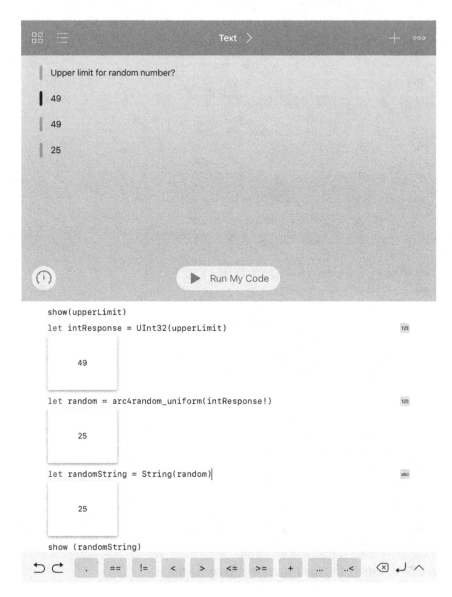

Figure 5-7. *Shows viewers for the playground as it runs*

Remember that Swift is strict with types so you need to convert strings to integers and vice versa - it doesn't happen automatically unless it is unambiguously possible. This helps to keep Swift code robust. In addition to the type conversions, note, too, that `intResponse` is an optional that needs to be unwrapped with !. (In production code, you would be safer to unwrap it with ? so that it will fail instead of crash if there is a `nil` there. In Chapter 7, in the section "Handling Data That Isn't There," you'll find out more about optionals.)

Go wrap up this section, and you can rename the Answer playground Random. Display the shelf of playgrounds and then press and hold the Answers playground. You'll be able to rename it as you see in Figure 5-8.

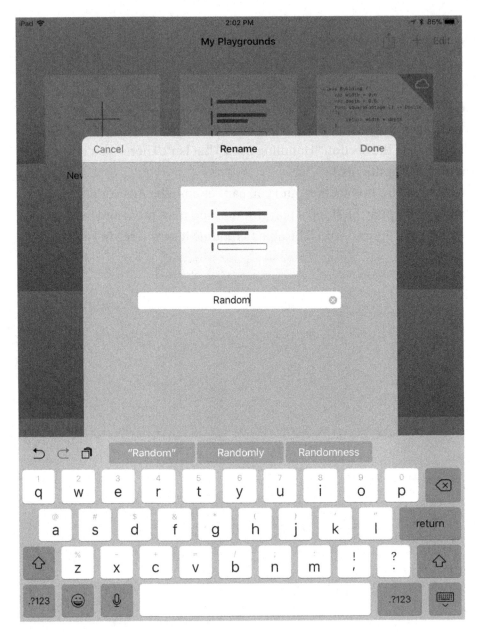

Figure 5-8. *Rename the playground to Random*

Creating Many Random Numbers

Remember that the purpose of creating random numbers in this chapter is to create a collection of meaningless (random) data that you can use to experiment with as you explore control management in code. It's easy to modify the Random playground to create several random numbers at a time. Just add the following lines of code to create 6 random numbers.

You already have the code to create and show a single random number. (Here is is again in case you need it here.)

```
var random = arc4random_uniform(intResponse!)
var randomString = String(random)
show (randomString)
```

You can add to that code to create another random number:

```
random = arc4random_uniform(intResponse!)
randomString = String(random)
show (randomString)
```

The only change you have to make is to remember that the original code declares variables as constants with let. Change the declarations to var so you can change their values, and in the subsequent calls, omit the type. Figure 5-9 shows the playground that now creates two random numbers (159 and 173) from the same intResponse.

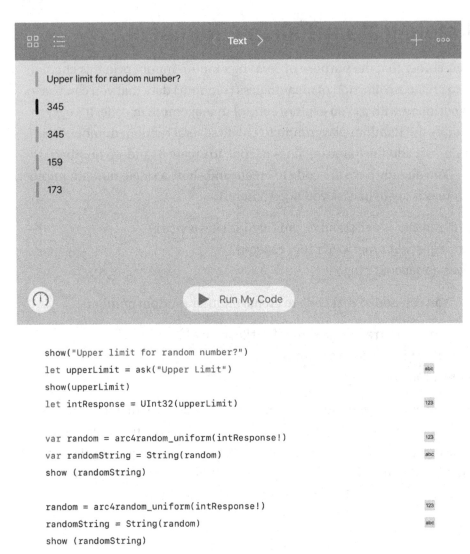

```
show("Upper limit for random number?")
let upperLimit = ask("Upper Limit")                          abc
show(upperLimit)
let intResponse = UInt32(upperLimit)                         123

var random = arc4random_uniform(intResponse!)                123
var randomString = String(random)                            abc
show (randomString)

random = arc4random_uniform(intResponse!)                    123
randomString = String(random)                                abc
show (randomString)
```

Figure 5-9. *Create multiple random numbers*

Create a Repetition Loop

This cut-and-paste method obviously doesn't scale well. Programming languages typically implement a variety of loops to do repetitive tasks. Repetition is a core principle of Computer Science. There are a number of types of repetition that you can choose from with most programming languages (including Swift).

All of the repetition structures have two primary components:

- There is a section of code that is subject to repetition. It can be a single line of code, several lines, or calls to one or more functions.

- There are controls for the repetition; basically, this determines how many times the process is repeated. Rather than a specific number of times, it can be conditional so that the repetition continues until that condition changes.

Note   This chapter shows you how to produce multiple random numbers: that is a basic use of repetition. Note that functional programming (described in Chapter 10 shows another way of handling repetition.)

Creating the Code to Repeat

Using the common repetition structure described here, you can set up the loop to create multiple random numbers. The code to start is shown in Listing 5-1. It asks for the upper limit of random numbers, converts the input (a string) into an integer (`UInt32`), and then calls the random number generator (`arc4random_uniform(intResponse!)`)

After the code executes the first time, it needs to create the second random number as in the previous listing. To repeat multiple times, you can cut and paste that code. (Remember that the first time through you set the variables, so it's the *second* time code that you repeat as shown in Figure 5-9.

Creating the Repetition Control (Limit)

The other part of repetition is the mechanism for controlling it. The logic of a loop like this in Swift is to use a variable to count the number of times you've been through the loop.

You can name the counter something imaginative and creative like i. Make certain that it is a var, because you will need to update it each time you go through the loop. Set it initially to 0.

```
var i = 0
```

Each time you go through the repetition loop, you will create a new random number and increment counter. The easiest way to do this in Swift is with the += counter, which is a *compound assignment* operator. It adds a value to a variable and assigns the added value to the variable. If you have a variable x that is set to 4, this code will set it to 5.

```
x += 1
```

That is the most common use, but you can also use x += 4.2 if your variable is a Double.

You do this in a *while* loop, which continues processing while its value is true. Thus, to execute the loop three times, set x to 0, add one to it each time you go through the while loop, and continue until the value of x is no longer less than 3.

Put all of this together, and you have a loop that can run 3 times as shown in Listing 5-1.

Listing 5-1. Create 3 Random Numbers

```
let prompt = ask("Upper limit for random number")
let intResponse = UInt32(prompt)

var random = arc4random_uniform(intResponse!)
var randomString = String(random)
show (randomString)

var i = 0

while i < 3 {
    i += 1
    random = arc4random_uniform(intResponse!)
    randomString = String(random)
    show (randomString)
}
```

The results are shown in Figure 5-10.

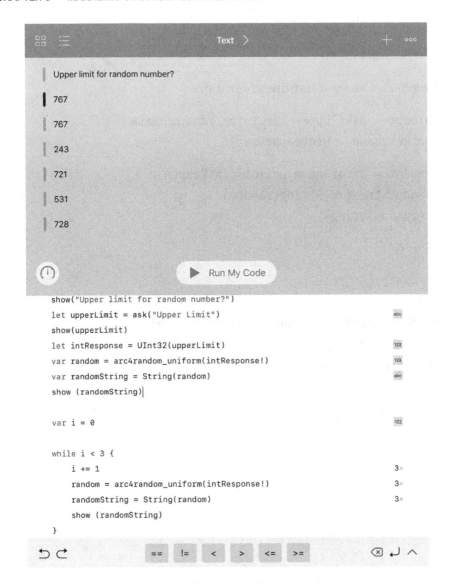

Figure 5-10. *Generating random numbers in a loop*

Because you are not generating printed output, you don't waste resources by printing output on paper. Try changing 3 to 10000 to produce 10,000 random numbers. (Remember not to use the comma when entering 10000 as code). You'll see the results go by very quickly.

To speed things up, don't show the result each time. Comment out the show statement as follows

```
//show (randomString)
```

In order to see when your 10,000 iteration loop finishes, add a final statement outside the brackets of the loop so that the last three lines look like this:

```
show (randomString) }
show ("Done")
```

Things will go even faster!

There's an important lesson to be learned here about just how fast and powerful the processors on mobile devices are today. A lot of the tips and "best practices" that you may find in older computer science books and texts, you'll find many ways to economize on the use of processors and storage. Those tips are still relevant, but the scales have changed and you need to apply them in more extreme cases.

Summary

This chapter shows you the basics of repetition control flow. You see how to set up a basic repetition in a Swift playground to generate 10,000 random numbers quickly. The basics of repetition control flow apply to many other types of processes; you'll see them throughout this book.

CHAPTER 6

Working with Data: Collections

In Chapter 5, you saw how to use repetition to create data - lots of it if you followed the example to create 10,000 random numbers. The question may have occurred to you: Why? What will you do with all that data that you created with the repetition code?

Computers and computer science frequently join together to do useful things. Neither data on its own without computation nor computation without data is generally very useful. In this chapter you see how to put the data you created in Chapter 5 into a usable collection. Later on in Chapter 9 ("Storing Data and Sharing Data"), you'll see how to make your data even more useful than it will be in this chapter.

Remember that the constructs and principles that are the backbone of computer science are there to make it easier to develop and maintain software. Successful developers look for ways to incorporate existing concepts and implementations into their product. That means less code to write, debug, and maintain. So don't just look at collections as tools to use to implement your ideas. Rather, look at ways in which to mold your ideas to take advantage of collections and other concepts so that there's less work for you to do.

© Jesse Feiler 2018
J. Feiler, *Learn Computer Science with Swift*, https://doi.org/10.1007/978-1-4842-3066-4_6

Using Types

Whether taken as single items or as collections, computer data is *typed*. Each data element that an app uses has a *type* that is assigned by the developer. Programming languages from almost the beginning have used types to convert the bits of digital storage into numbers of various sorts. The simplest conversion takes all of the bits in a computer word and uses their on/off status to create a binary number. Depending on the number of bits in a computer word, the binary number can range from 0 to a very large number.

Very early in the development of computers and computer science, it became obvious that this conversion of bits to a binary number wasn't nearly enough. A common solution was to take a bit at the high end of the binary number and reserve it for a special purpose: a minus sign. Thus both positive and negative numbers could be stored.

Further refinements included storing a single set of bits in a word as if they were two separate integers. This allowed the representation of floating-point numbers with one integer representing the *significand* (sometimes called the *mantissa*) and the other representing the exponent for the power of ten that will create the appropriate value when it is used to multiply the significand. All of this is done with software - the actual words of storage remain just a row of bits. Because conversions from one type of number can be done easily, they are done all the time in software. Often neither developer nor user is aware of this.

There are details about using built-in types as well as types that are created by Swift in the following chapter. For now, just be aware that types are constructs that convert the physical bits in a computer word to something with meaning to developers, users, and normal people.

Scalar Data

The simplest form of data is a *scalar* or *variable* - a single data element that is basically the same as a simple algebraic term as in

$$x = 15$$

You will often find descriptions and definitions of scalars as the contents of a single memory location. In fact, most of the time data is stored in *words* that are collections of *bits*. The hardware handles these words very efficiently as it stores and retrieves the contents of words.

When a computer word is 64 bits long, it can theoretically store 64 separate yes/no (Boolean) values. Hardware and software let you access the word as a single value (usually a number) by the individual bits. You can go further to access the bits in a word in groups that often correspond to letters.

Moving On to Collected Data

Storing one number in a single computer word that is referenced by a simple variable (a *scalar*) is a good way of keeping track of data that you calculate or read in. You can then use the basic operations described in other chapters of this book to manipulate the data and create more data in other formats and styles.

Modern programming languages support various collections of data. The most basic of these is an *array* - a numbered list of items (perhaps the names of students in a classroom). Another common type of collection is a *set* - a collection of items that is not a list ("set" is used in the sense in which it is used in logic and mathematics). Swift implements both arrays and sets.

There is another type of collection called *dictionary* in Swift and *associative array* in languages such as PHP. Whereas the items in an array make up a numbered list, items in a dictionary are identified by strings or other types.

Arrays are the oldest and most basic collections in computer science. Sets are the next oldest, and dictionaries (associative arrays) are the most recent. This chapter examines each of these in chronological order.

All are subclasses of `Collection`, and most use the same basic methods that are described first in arrays in this section. Note that these classes are in `Foundation`, so you must use either of these import statements in your Swift code of Playground:

```
import Foundation
import UIKit
```

It is always a good practice to import the smallest number of frameworks possible. `UIKit` imports `Foundation` automatically, but if you only need Foundation, import it explicitly and don't worry about importing the code you don't need in `UIKit`. Xcode and the build process will strip it out if it's not needed, but it's better just to import what you need to begin with.

Using Arrays

Arrays in any computer language are basically ordered lists. A list of students in a class is not ordered, but an alphabetized list is ordered.

Although arrays are ordered lists, sometimes the order is irrelevant. For example, a list of students that is not ordered still contains all students in the class. You don't have to use the ordering in your code.

The numbering and ordering of elements in an array is handled by the array construct itself: the numbers of individual items are not in the items themselves unless you put them there. If you do, you can have items like the ones shown in Table 6-1. Note that in Table 6-1 the indexes are integers and the contents can be anything. The first two are strings, and the last one is an integer (note the absence of quotes around it).

Table 6-1. *Sample array*

Index	Contents
0	"Content 17"
1	"Data for item 32"
2	2

Arrays of one sort or another are available in almost every programming language and operating system. They enable you to store and retrieve data in a basic way; in addition, they make it easy to repeat processes for the elements of an array.

As you delve into computer science, you will notice that concepts such as arrays are the building blocks that you use. As is the case with arrays, you'll find some basic features of these building blocks. (In the case of arrays, it's the basic principle that an array is an ordered list of elements indexed as part of the data array rather than by elements within the array.)

Features beyond the basics have been implemented many times by developers and designers who use programming languages to expand on the basic structure. Over time, many of these enhancements and additions have gradually moved into the programming languages and operating systems. It is unfortunately true that many people continue to focus on the initial building blocks and the individually crafted enhancements to it.

Swift itself incorporates many enhancements to basic arrays and their functionality. This section discusses many of the things you can do with arrays - most of which are built directly into Swift.

Experienced developers and designers know that using these features in languages such as Swift is the path to successful code. The simplest way to avoid bugs is not to write your own code, and the code that's already written in Swift and related frameworks has been written, tested, and proven in use in some cases for decades if you include the Cocoa and Cocoa Touch frameworks.

In the sections of this chapter that relate to arrays, the following topics are covered:

- Basic Terminology

- Indexing Array Elements

- Swift Arrays and Types

- Declaring and Creating Arrays

- Modifying a `var` Array

- Multi-Dimensional Arrays

- Finding Array Elements

- Adding and Deleting Array Elements

- Looping Through an Array

Basic Terminology

These are terms that are commonly used in talking about arrays.

- The contents of an array are called *items* or *elements*.

- The ordering of an array is governed by one or more *indexes*.

- Items in an array are written with *subscripts* that identify the element or item by its numerical position in the array.

- In many languages including Swift, arrays are written with their subscripts in square brackets as in `myArray` [3], which would be item number three in `myArray`.

Indexing Array Elements

As you see in Table 6-1, the array handles indexes, and you do whatever you want with the contents of the array. Notice that the default index numbers start at zero. This is a legacy of the original implementation of arrays. In many cases, an array location was the first element of the array (often the first word of storage), and the index is the distance from the first element's memory location. Thus, the first element (which you might think of element number 1) has no distance from the first element because it *is* the first element.

Some languages allow you to start indexing your array at a number other than zero but, in fact, the language and operating system itself perform the manipulations to convert the 0-based index to a different base.

And, just to make things more interesting, the physical storage of an array may not be consecutive memory locations today, but arrays start at zero because they always have started at zero.

There are no gaps in arrays. Thus, if you look at Table 6-1 and were to delete the item at index 1, the array would look like Table 6-2. The old index 1 item is gone, and the previous index 2 item becomes index 1.

Table 6-2. *Sample array with a row deleted*

Index	Contents
0	"Content 17"
1	2

Note   See "Finding Array Elements" later in this chapter to see how to locate array elements by content rather than by index.

Swift Arrays and Types

Arrays in Swift are typed. That means that the elements of an array all have a common type. You can create an array of integers, an array of strings, or an array of any other type.

Having a single type in an array can make for some efficiencies in code generation as well as others at runtime. (Furthermore, it can make your code more robust because improperly mixing types within an array can be flagged by the compiler rather than generating a runtime error.)

Of course, having a single type in an array can also be inconvenient in some ways. Swift manages this with its hierarchy of types. As you will see in Chapter 7, Swift types include basic types such as integers as well as special types Any and AnyObject. Thus, you can create an array of Any, which could include integers as well as strings.

It is a best practice in Swift to use the most restrictive types you can use. Yes, you could create all of your arrays as Any? (that is, optional versions of any type at all), but that bypasses all the checking and optimization that is built in.

Declaring and Creating Arrays

In languages such as Swift, you must declare variables before you use them. (This is different from languages such as PHP in which you can create variables as you need them just by using them.)

Arrays are no different from any other symbols in Swift: you declare them before you use them. Declarations of variables include their name along with a modifier that determines if the variables is modifiable (var) or not (let).

Because an array is typed, you commonly declare it with its type. There are two forms of syntax you can use.

The first method is to simply declare the array type as in:

```
Array <Int>
```

You can also declare a variable with both a name and a type that will be an array using syntax such as this:

```
var intArray:[Int]
```

This is a normal declaration; the type following the colon is an array of `Ints`.

This is just the declaration. If you attempt to use it you will get an error message that it has not been initialized. Remember that there are two steps to creating and using a variable or constant: the declaration must be followed by initialization.

You can initialize an array just as you would initialize an instance of a class or other elements in Swift. You add () after the name. This code initializes the array:

```
intArray = [Int]()
```

You can declare, initialize, and print out the array in a Swift playground as you see in Figure 6-1.

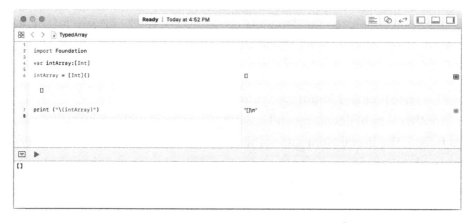

Figure 6-1. *Declare and initialize an array*

Elements of an array are enclosed in square brackets. In Figure 6-1, you can see that the array is empty. It is an opening and closing bracket. With additional spacing, here is what the array looks like:

```
[    ]
```

You can combine the declaration and initialization of an array with the following syntax:

```
var intArray2 = [Int]()
```

Figure 6-2 shows this syntax in action. As you can see, once again you have created an empty array. (The debug area at the bottom of the window is the best place to see that the results are identical.)

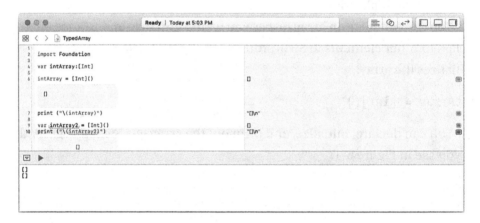

Figure 6-2. *Declare and initialize an array in one line of code*

This style is called *initializer syntax.*

Another way of declaring and creating an array is with an *array literal:* that is, with the literal elements of the array. In this style, you declare the array with its type;

```
var intArray3 : [Int]
```

Then, to create the array you simply list the elements in square brackets:

```
var intArray3 : [Int] = [2, 3, 5, 7, 11]
```

You see this in Figure 6-3.

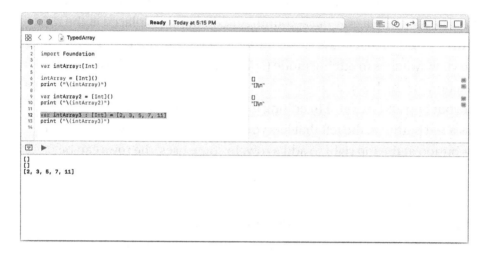

Figure 6-3. *Declare and initialize an array with literals*

When you declare an array with literals, Swift can infer the type of the array from the literals you provide.

Modifying a **var** array

There are three ways you can modify a var array:

- You can modify the array structure itself. That is, you can add or delete elements from the array.

- You can modify the elements themselves so that they contain different data values but the number of elements remains the same.

- You can also do both.

101

In some languages the two types of modification are treated differently. You can see this in the UITableViewController class of iOS and in apps that use it.

Figure 6-4 shows the default behavior or `UITableViewController`. At the left, you see a table view with rows grouped into sections; each section has a header with a gray background. An Edit button is placed at the right of the navigation bar at the top of the view. If you tap the Edit button, the view switches to editing mode (specifically, it calls the `setEditing` function in which you actually handle the transition to and from edit mode for your app and its data).In editing mode (shown on the right), each row has a red button at the left that lets you delete it. The developer can add a + button at the top right to add a row. In some uses, the rows can be rearranged.

Note   The screenshots in this section are from The Nonprofit Risk App on the App Store at `https://itunes.apple.com/us/app/np-risk/id1262903630?ls=1&mt=8`.

All of these operations modify the array and its structure: they do not affect the array's data. Although, if a row is deleted, its data is deleted so in that case the data is modified. The typical implementation of this type of interface provides for the editing of the array itself as shown in Figure 6-4, which shows the table view on the left and the table view in edit mode on the right. If you tap on an item in the list you then move to the detail data for that item as you see in Figure 6-5. Note that there is a new Edit button at the top right of the detail view. This controls editing of the detail view - the content of the array elements.

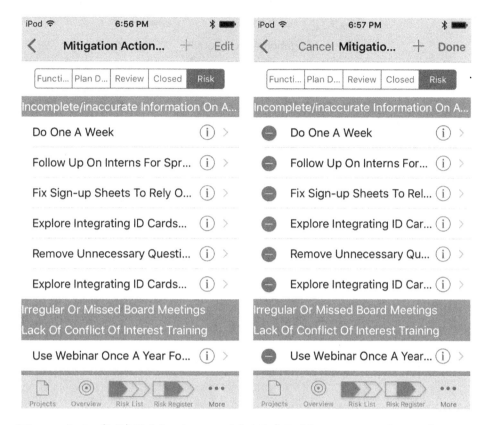

Figure 6-4. (left) Table view and (right) Table view in edit mode

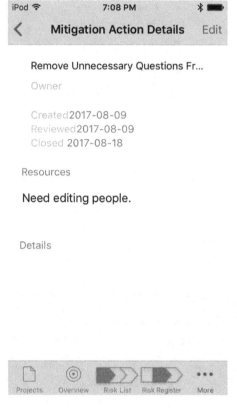

Figure 6-5. *Editing the detail data of an array element*

Multi-Dimensional Arrays

Arrays often have more than one dimension. A two-dimensional array can handle data from a spreadsheet very easily. Such an array has two indexes - one for rows and one for columns. Arrays can have a number of dimensions in most languages.

For example, you could have an array representing customer transactions. The first dimension might be customer data (name and address for example). The next dimension might be for individual transactions (with a date and amount). Then it might follow the dimension of payments. You can't do this in Swift, and, as you start thinking about it, you may find it difficult to manage the multiple dimensions.

In any language, this kind of multi-dimensional array quickly becomes unwieldy. We have other data structures that can more easily handle this type of data. In Swift, you'll find other types of collections such as sets and dictionaries that can organize data into specific types of collections. The single dimension of a swift array can itself contain other arrays, dictionaries, or sets; that dimension could also contain tuples that are yet another way of organizing data within a single entity which can be stored in an array. (Tuples are discussed in the following chapter.)

So don't let the one-dimensional aspect of Swift arrays trouble you until you have seen these other features of the language.

Finding Array Elements

Each element in an array can be accessed using its index. The first item in an array is array[0] — remember arrays start at zero. However, as you insert and delete elements, the indexes change so that the array has no gaps. This means that what is index number 52 today may be index 35 tomorrow (and may not even be there the next day).

Swift (like a number of other languages) solves this issue for you by letting you locate an array element by its content rather than by its index. The code is shown in Figure 6-6.

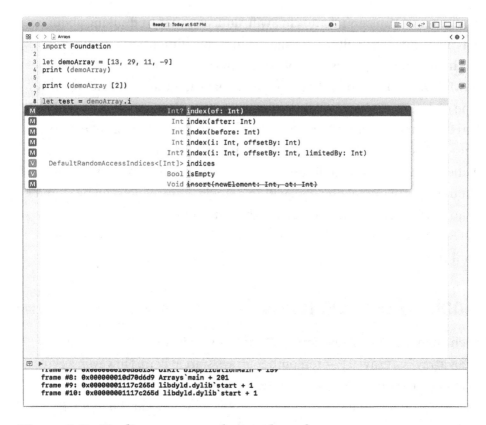

Figure 6-6. *Finding an array element by value*

You create an array with its values using

```
let demoArray = [13, 29, 11, -9]
```

In Figure 6-6, you can see that you can print the entire array with

```
print (demoArray)
```

You can get the third element (index 2) with

```
print (demoArray[2])
```

You can use the method index(of:) to find an element. Notice in the code completion of Figure 6-6 that code completion expects an Int as the argument. Nowhere did you declare the array as an array of Ints; the parser has inferred that from the values you entered.

If you enter the values shown in Figure 6-7, a Double is inferred.

Figure 6-7. *Swift infers an array of Doubles when appropriate*

When you complete the code, the playground runs as you see in Figure 6-8.

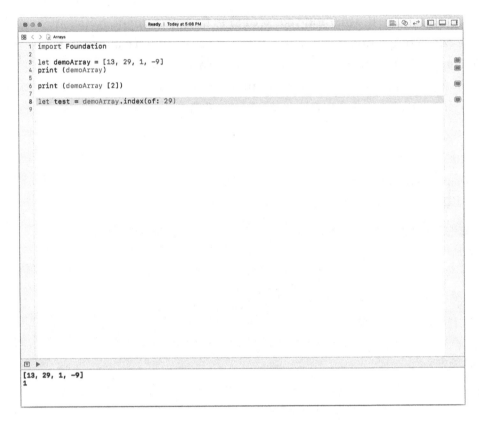

Figure 6-8. *Create and print arrays in a Swift playground*

Tip   index(of:) and the code completion can be very useful. Just start typing as shown in Figures 6-6 and 6-7 to see how Swift has handled type inference. If you happened to create an array of Int based on your initial data and you want to eventually add a float or Double, declare it with the type as in let demoArray:Double = [3, 29, 1, -9] This will create an array of Doubles even though the initial values are Ints.

Adding and Deleting Array Elements

Adding and deleting array elements after you have first created it is not complicated. The easiest way to get started is with code completion. Begin by checking that your array's declaration is var so that you can modify it. (It might be let if you declared it with constants.)

If you think that the method you need is add, code completion will balk. It's append, and if you try that, you'll see that it works, and, as you see in Figure 6-9, an Int is expected.

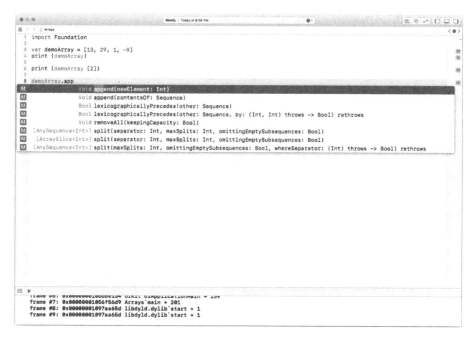

Figure 6-9.   *Start to append a new array element*

After you append the new array element, the playground runs as you see in Figure 6-10.

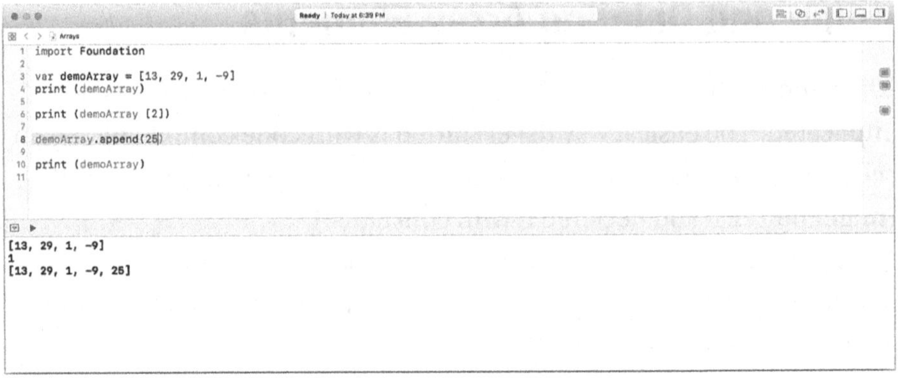

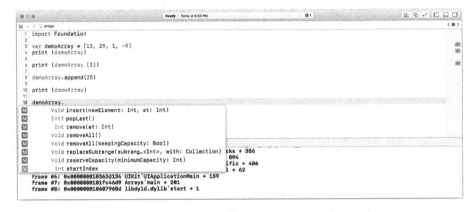

Figure 6-10. *Append elements to a* var *array*

You'll notice that appending adds elements at the end of the array. There are a variety of additional methods in Swift that you can use. It's easy to use code completion and just scroll down to find relevant methods as you see in Figure 6-11.

Figure 6-11. *Use code completion to see other array methods*

Of course, you can also use Help ➤ API reference in Xcode or developer.apple.com. Note that you can see methods to insert new elements at various places in the array or to remove elements. These are details of Swift and other languages, so you can explore the documentation.

The array principles are the same across languages and operating systems. The only major difference is that some languages do not provide as many built-in methods and functions to manipulate arrays. (Furthermore, some people prefer to write the array manipulation code themselves although that means more errors may be introduced into the code.)

Deleting an array element is simpler than adding one because you don't have to worry about keeping track of the new element and where it belongs in the array. To delete an array element, just locate it either by index or with one of the functions discussed in the previous section. To remove an element, use one of the following methods of an array:

```
arrayName.remove(at: Int)
arrayName.removeFirst()
arrayName.removeLast()
arrayName.removeFirst(n: Int) // to remove several first elements
arrayName.removeLast(n:Int)  // to remove several last elements
```

You can use `index(of:Int)` to find the index and then use `remove(at: Int)`.

Looping Through an Array

Often you want to access each of the elements of an array in turn. You may want to display the names of each student in a class, you may want to find the highest and lowest temperatures in a 24-hour period, you may want to do anything else that involves looping through each element of an array.

Note   Given an array of 10,000 random numbers (which you may have already created), you might want to calculate the average of the first 5,000 numbers and another average for the last 5,000 numbers. The closer those averages are, the more random the numbers are if they are all created as being between the same upper and lower bounds (such as 0 and 1.0). This is discussed in Chapter 8, "Managing Control Flow."

Using Sets

Sets are collections — subclasses of `Collection` just like arrays. They are the same sets that you encounter in set theory (a branch of mathematical logic). If you haven't read the previous section on arrays, you might want to at least skim it because many of the set concepts are the same as for arrays. (In fact, if you look at the documentation, you will find that many set and array methods (like dictionary methods you will see later in this chapter) are actually methods of `Collection`.

Sets have one critical feature that is the reason they are used in so many places in Swift apps. Yes, you can do various set theory operations on sets (unions, intersections, joins, and so forth — see "Working with Sets" later in this section.) What matters to many developers is that sets can be used in property lists (see Chapter 9, "Storing Data and Sharing Data"). You can place a collection of various elements, most commonly instances of classes or structures, into a set. At that point, the set can be used in a property list and it will be written to and read from a property list or other Cocoa/Cocoa Touch structures without any further coding on your part. So if you want to forget about set theory and manipulating sets but use them simply as a fast way to structure data to be stored and retrieved, you will not be alone. This is one of the most-used aspects of sets.

Other features of sets discussed in this section are the following:

- Basic Set Terminology

- Identifying and Finding Set Elements

- Declaring and Creating Swift Sets and Types

- Adding and Deleting Set Elements

- Working with Sets

Basic Set Terminology

Sets are collections of elements that have no order to them. They are unique. You cannot have two elements of a set that have the same value. In an array, you can have multiple elements with the same value because they also have unique indexes at any given moment (remember that those indexes can change as elements are added to or removed from the array, but at any given moment, the index is the way to access an array element regardless of its value).

Identifying and Finding Set Elements

Behind the scenes, the elements of a set are *hashed*. That is, a formula is applied to the contents in such as way as to create an integer that is unique to the data that has been hashed. It is this hashed value that is used to identify set elements. There is no need for a subscript or other identification. Because the hashed values are stored, there are no duplicates (that is, no two set elements can have the same hashed value). In order to access a set element, all you need is to know that the element is in the set. Once you know it is in the set, you need no further access mechanism.

Of course, you need to find out if it is a member of a set. There is a set function for that:

```
contains (_:)
```

It returns a `Bool`, so you can use it as in the following code:

```
let myElement = // something
if mySet.contains (myElement) {
  // go ahead and use it knowing that it's a member of the set
}
```

Declaring and Creating Swift Sets and Types

A set is declared using a type such as this:

```
Set<Int>
Set<String>
```

and so forth with the other basic Swift types including `Double` and `Bool`. You can create a set using syntax like this:

```
var mySet = Set<String>()
```

The set is created and empty.

As with arrays, you can use an array literal to create a set using syntax such as the following:

```
var mySet: Set<String> = ["mountain", "valley"]
```

This combines the basic type declaration with the creation of a variable that contains the set's initial data. Remember that if the set's type can be inferred from the initial elements, you can skip the type in the declaration, but if the initial elements might suggest a less inclusive type than you want, use the type declaration.

Adding and Deleting Set Elements

You can add an element to a set very simply as long as the new element adheres to two important rules for sets:

1. The element cannot already be in the set. Remember that set elements are unique.

2. The element must be of the type in the set declaration. (Remember that you have Any? and AnyObject? types you can use for tremendous flexibility.)

To add an element to a set (as long as it obeys the two rules), the most basic syntax is

```
insert(_:)
```

as in

```
mySet.insert(myNewElement)
```

The companion removal method is

```
remove(_:)
```

as in

```
mySet.remove(myNewElement)
```

Because sets are not ordered, you don't worry about where to insert the element (first, last, or so forth). You insert it into the set wherever it happens to go.

> **Tip**   When debugging code, remember that sets are unordered, but from time to time they may appear ordered because the order in which you have added or removed elements may appear to create an order but that is only a transient matter. From one execution of your app to another the order may change. Do not rely on accidental ordering that you may temporarily create while editing and debugging.

Working with Sets

The two basic set theory operations are supported with set methods in Swift:

```
aSet.union(anotherSet)
aSet.intersection(anotherSet)
```

Other methods support more advanced operations, but, as noted previously, many sets are created for their ability to be easily written and read. Their set theory operations aren't used in many cases.

> **Note**   See Chapter 8, "Managing Control Flow" for iterating through sets.

Using Dictionaries

Sets are totally unordered. Arrays are ordered by the sequence of items in them. Dictionaries are more sophisticated. One way of thinking about them is that they are ordered but not by numbers. With an array, you can reference an element that is the fifth element of the array (remember the array is zero-based) by using

```
myArray[6]
```

With a dictionary, you might use syntax such as

```
myDictionary["six"]
```

Associative arrays are implemented in many languages such as PHP, JavaScript, Python, Ruby, and Perl. In Swift and Objective-C, they are *dictionaries*.

- Basic Dictionary Terminology

- Declaring and Creating a Dictionary

- Adding and Deleting Dictionary Elements

Basic Dictionary Terminology

There is no ordering to set elements. Elements in an array are indexed, and the indexes are managed by the array itself. What is element number 5 today may be element 25 tomorrow depending on additions and deletions.

Dictionaries are collections of pairs of data: *keys* and *values* (*key-value pairs*). Commonly, keys are strings, but they need not be (in some languages dictionary or associative array keys must be strings).

Declaring and Creating a Dictionary

You can formally declare a dictionary in Swift with

```
Dictionary<Key, Value>
```

Key and Value are the types of keys and values in the dictionary.

The shorthand form omits the keyword Dictionary; you can declare a dictionary with

```
[Key: Value]
```

Again, Key and Value are the types of keys and values in the dictionary.

You can create an empty dictionary using ( ) after the declaration as in

`Dictionary <Int, String>()`

This declaration deliberately reverses a common dictionary structure in which the key is a string. Here, the key is an `Int` and the value is a `string`. That shows you the options available to you.

If you forget the ( ) when you intend to create a dictionary, Fix-It will remind you as you see in Figure 6-12.

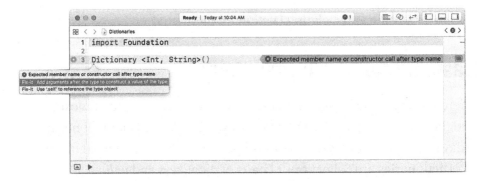

Figure 6-12. *Declaring and creating a dictionary*

Tip   If you use dictionaries, you must import `Foundation` in your app or playground. If you are importing UIKit, you don't need to import Foundation as well because it is included in UIKit.

You can assign a newly declared and created dictionary to a variable using code such as

`var testDictionary = Dictionary <Int, String>()`

If you tap the viewer in line 3 of Figure 6-13, you'll see how Swift Playgrounds reports it:

`[:]`

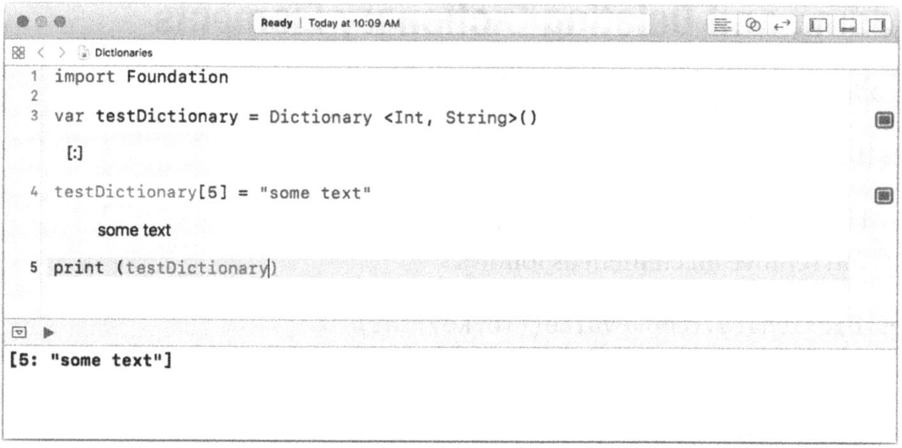

```
●●●                        Ready | Today at 10:09 AM              ≡ ⊘ ↵  □ □ □
⊞ < >  Dictionaries
1  import Foundation
2
3  var testDictionary = Dictionary <Int, String>()             ▣

     [:]

4  testDictionary[5] = "some text"                             ▣

       some text

5  print (testDictionary)

▽ ▶
[5: "some text"]
```

Figure 6-13. *Assign a dictionary to a* var

Dictionary entries are enclosed in square brackets with a colon separating the key and value. An empty dictionary has only the square brackets and the colon as you see.

You can also create a dictionary from a *dictionary literal* that functions much as an array literal does. It is enclosed in square brackets and contains comma-separated key-value pairs.

As an example, assume you want to create this dictionary:

```
"Breakfast":"Eggs"
"Lunch": "Soup"
"Dinner": "Vegetables and Rice"
```

You can create it with a dictionary literal as in:

```
var menu = ["Breakfast":"Eggs", "Lunch":"Soup",
"Dinner":"Vegetables and Rice"]
```

Adding and Deleting Dictionary Elements

To add a dictionary element, insert it into the dictionary with its key as:

```
testDictionary [5] = "some text"
```

This is shown on line 4 of Figure 6-13.
You remove an element as follows

```
testDictionary.removeValue((forKey:Int)
```

As shown in Figure 6-14, code completion inserts the appropriate type for the key depending on how you have declared the dictionary.

Figure 6-14. *Remove a dictionary element*

Summary

This chapter shows you the basics collections in Swift and in computer science in general. The constructs are basically the same in all languages although some (such as associative arrays and dictionaries or sets) may not be implemented in some special-purpose languages.

All collections let you handle collections of data as a single entity. For example, a set containing many elements can read or written with a single line of code in Swift. Furthermore, you can use collections where single variables are required. In a dictionary, for example, there can only be one element for a given key. However, if that element is itself a collection (an array, set, or dictionary), that entire collection can be part of another collection. You'll see more on this in the following chapters.

CHAPTER 7

Working with Data: Types

One of the basics of computer science is the concept of *data types*. In the simplest case, a type is a way of interpreting the digital bits in a computer's memory or in a data stream for or from a storage device. Bits have one of two values (on/off), and they are typically grouped together logically into *bytes*. Bytes began as collections of bits that could represent a single character; the first implementations were of six bits, but today bytes are typically either bits so that more characters can be represented by a single byte.

It is important to note that while bits are physical items, bytes are logical collections. They are assembled and interpreted by hardware and software based on the underlying bits.

The bits (the hardware) are physically collected into *words* that typically can contain enough bits to form several characters, but, remember, the assembling of bits into bytes is logical and not physical while the assembling of bits into words is done in hardware.

Words can be accessed directly in software, which is what programs and operating systems do all the time. You can use software to look inside a word to work with individual bits and bytes.

© Jesse Feiler 2018
J. Feiler, *Learn Computer Science with Swift*, https://doi.org/10.1007/978-1-4842-3066-4_7

This chapter shows you what happens as words (physical groups of bits) and bytes (logical groups of bits) are used by the operating system and, through it, by users. One of the basic ways in which words are managed is by grouping then into data types. This chapter explores data types and how you can use them. The main topics covered in this chapter are the following:

- Why Types Matter

- Basic Types

- Working with Tuples

- Advanced Swift Types

- Creating New Types

- Handling Data That Isn't There (Optionals)

Why Types Matter

The basics of types are simple. They are the primary intermediary between the on/off bits in storage and data flows and the higher-level constructs such as bits and bytes as well as the even-higher constructs that bits and bytes form.

If that were all that types did, that would be enough (as it was in the very earliest computers). It's a critical link between the hardware and the software. Computer science goes beyond the basics of how computers work. It encompasses the concepts that let computers and people perform useful work and communicate with one another. From that point of view, types have another critical role to play.

A type provides the rules for assembling bits into words that can be used. Those words can have types assigned to them (the usage is that the words are *typed*). Those typed words are then used in code. Remember that types are logical constructs — the physical words never change no matter what type they are used as. (The data within the words change.)

By referring to a word as a specific type, compilers can perform one of their most critical roles. Languages and compilers support varying amounts of *type safety*. Type safety is the set of rules that determines how a word of a given type can be used in conjunction with other types. If the combination of types is logically impossible according to the type safety rules, it is caught as an error by the compiler, and the code won't run. This is an important role for the compiler to play, because the alternative is to just go ahead and do something that is illogical and watch as the app crashes.

It is generally considered a good thing for coders to get the errors rather than letting users get them.

Types and type safety make this possible.

You can mix types in various ways depending on the rules for each type. For example, you can divide two integers by one another (5 divided by 2, for example). The result that you probably want is a floating point number (2.5).

Depending on the context, Swift, Xcode, or the runtime environment will either refuse to perform an illegal operation (that is, it will get an error), or it will warn you about performing a possibly illogical operation (that is usually implemented with a warning to you, the coder).

A key part of implementing type safety is allowing developers to convert one type to another (this is called type *coercion*). Sometimes, the format of a number itself can serve as an indicator of its type. For example, 2 is an integer both in common usage and in Swift. 2.0 is a floating point number (note the decimal point). Its value is the same as 2 (without a decimal point), but it is of a different type.

Note   Swift supports two kinds of floating point numbers. Float is stored in such a way that it may have as few as 6 places to the right of the decimal point. Double is stored with much greater precision. Double is the preferred and default type for floating point numbers.

Looking at Stacks and Heaps

Types describe how the bits in a word should be interpreted — be it as an integer, floating point number, one or more characters or bytes, or even the collection of individual bits that can be accessed as on/off values on their own.

However, not everything you deal with in an app consists of words like these. As you saw in Chapter 6, 'Working with Data: Collections," you also need to deal with collections of data. Most of the time, these collections are collections of words that are interpreted as certain types. As you will see in Chapter 10, "Building Components," sometimes you deal with objects. Collections and objects don't fit inside single words, so another type of storage is needed. For items like these, operating systems typically reserve a section of memory in which they can place these large and often variably sized items.

Storing Data at Runtime

Where data is stored at runtime becomes a critical issue in designing operating systems and compilers. It is largely — but not totally — handled for you behind the scenes. Because it is not totally handled for you, you need to know the basic concepts of runtime storage, and that is described in this section. You'll also see how it all fits together so that you as a developer can provide the functionality and responsiveness that users expect from modern software and development techniques.

In the first days of computers (mainframe computers in the 1940s), one program ran at a time. The entire computer was dedicated to running that program. All of its resources (storage, communication channels, and printers) were devoted to the program that was running. Among the resources devoted to that single program were the computer itself and its operators. If you wanted to run a program in most environments, you made an appointment. It was a far cry from picking up an iPhone and tapping an app; these appointments were often scheduled for a time slot sometime in the future. If your project was not a high priority, your time slot might be 2:30 a.m. next Thursday.

This type of operation made a number of things much easier than they are in today's world. For one thing, with the entire computer available to a single program, that meant all of its memory was dedicated to that program with only a fairly small piece of that memory devoted to overhead and maintenance of the computer (although the billing could be done manually on cards or pages in a loose-leaf binder).

Now that people expect to run multiple apps at the same time on a mobile device, it's impossible to dedicate all of the device's memory to a single app. People wouldn't stand for that. "What do you mean I can't watch a movie while I make a phone call and design a poster! I paid extra for 256 gigs of storage! Where did it go? I'm going to take my iPhone to an Apple Genius Bar and have them open it up to verify that someone didn't cheat me on my gigs."

In order to make the most of the memory available in any device (this goes back decades to the beginnings of time sharing in the 1960s), multiple programs could run at the same time so that as resources like printers or data storage devices were needed the program could be set aside with all its data until the device was ready. Throughput was faster even though there was time required to swap programs and data in and out. This is the same basic model that we use today (this is a very basic overview).

Programs began to be structured in such a way that a discrete set of code could execute from start to finish with the data that it needed. When that set of code was completed, it and its data were simply discarded — this is not the swapping in and out of programs and data to maximize the use of resources. Rather, it is a separate type of requesting, using, and then discarding memory. Both of these processes are necessary to make the most of computers and their resources.

Stacks and Queues

The word *stack* is used frequently in computer science. It is used in its simple everyday sense of a pile of things (often a stack of paper, but sometimes a stack of bricks or other objects). As is the case with everyday stacks, you add items to the stack by placing them on top. The easiest way of taking items off a stack is to take the topmost item. In computer science, this is referred to as a last in-first out stack (sometimes referred to as *LIFO*).

With a stack, no matter how many items are in the stack, it's really only the top one (the last in/first out item) that needs to be accessed. The action of adding items to the top of a stack and removing them from the top of a stack is called *pushing* (pushing a new item onto the top of a stack) and *popping* (removing the top item from the top of a stack).

The order of items in a stack is important.

A related concept to stacks is the concepts of *queues*. That, too, is an ordered list of items, and you can also add items to the top of a queue. However, with a queue, it is not the top item (the last added) that is the first to be removed. Instead, with a queue you add items to the top (as in a stack), but you remove items from the bottom. This is a last in-last out (*LILO*) structure. You see this type of queue in action in many cases every day. In a supply cabinet, you may store items in such a way that you use the oldest items first.

The order of items in a queue is just as important as in a stack.

Note   The following is a simplified overview of memory management designed to help you understand the basic principles. Modern computers have significant enhancements and optimizations beyond these basics.

Inside the computer as an app runs, the data that is required for a section of code (a function or procedure in many cases, but this applies to any section of code), is pushed onto a stack. This means that as the function or procedure starts to run, memory storage for each of the variables needed by the code is set aside for the lifetime of the code. All of the data is located together. When the section of code is finished, all of the data set aside for the variables can be released to the system. This is called *cutting back the stack*, and it is a critical way of reusing the memory of a computer.

This way of optimizing memory use relies on being able to identify the memory locations needed for the operation of a section of code. When that code starts to run, whatever memory will be needed for its variables is set aside (*allocated*) even if the variables are not yet in use. This assures that the code can run to completion without running out of memory.

Heaps

Stacks are a simple way of organizing and reusing memory, but there's one big problem: not all data fits nicely onto a stack of computer words. Many data structures are much bigger than a single word. The simplest example of these are the collections discussed in Chapter 6. Almost every computer language has its collection types, and storing them has always been a challenge. One way it is addressed has been to place a computer word on the stack that has a special meaning — it is a reference to the actual data that is placed elsewhere in the computer's memory. (This method of handling arrays goes back to the 1950s.) By using such references, you can continue the basic idea of cutting back a stack. It is just a little bit more complicated because the operating system has to recognize that when it cuts back an array reference word from the stack, it must release the associated memory for the array in question.

All of this can work well even though it takes some time and processing power to handle the references. An array is declared in a procedure, method, or function and its elements are referenced somewhere else in memory. The "somewhere" else is referred to commonly as the *heap*. That's just what it is — an unstructured heap of data. When the data for an array or other structured item is stored in the heap via a reference from the stack, things are relatively easy to manage.

The big problem arises when there is data in the heap that is not associated with a stack reference word. This situation is handled with yet another strategy. The operating system still uses reference words on the stack to refer to unstructured data in the heap, but there's a new element added to the process. The operating system keeps track of the *number* of reference words pointing to some data in the heap. In the case of a reference word on the stack, there's only one reference: the one from the stack. However, when there is shared data, this unstructured data on the heap may be referred to by many references throughout your app. When the operating system notices that the number of references to the data decreases to zero, it can reuse that memory space.

All of this requires the operating system to keep track of the stacks (for each app that's running); storage in the heap; and, in the case of mobile devices, constant changes in location as well as phone calls; messages; tweets; and everything else that's going on in those devices. The amount of storage and processing power that are used for these operations are significant in any computer.

Tip   All of this work that is done behind the scenes on any computer is most successful when users don't know that it's even happening. However, when you are considering configuring a computer (or buying a new one), these resources have to be factored into your requirements. Having enough storage space for your library of a thousand songs and nothing more is not going to leave you with a functioning computer.

Basic Types

The basic types for most computer languages represent numbers, characters, and strings in various ways. Although the storage is ultimately one or more computer words, the distinctions among these types are implemented in software — the operating system and the apps that run on computers. Computer words are basically interchangeable. In fact, one of the great breakthroughs in the development of compilers and computer languages was the realization that the data stored in and manipulated by a computer could be what we normally would consider data (numbers, for example) andit could also be computer instructions (add two numbers perhaps).

There is another type of storage that is used behind the scenes in computer systems. Words can contain internal operational data and instructions that are required for the operation of the computer itself. For example, reference words (described in the previous section) are stored in the same physical words that could otherwise be used for traditional data, but the operating system makes certain that such data is protected from unauthorized manipulation by apps and users.

Numeric Storage

There are two was to store numbers: they can be stored as integers (whole numbers) or numbers with a fractional component (commonly referred to by various names such as *decimal numbers*, which is actually a misleading term in some cases).

Using Integers

Integer numbers are simple numbers. You can convert the bits in a computer word into a base-2 number and there you have a number that can be converted into any other base, but the most common conversion is from base 2 to base 10.

Computers typically use almost an entire word to store integers. "Almost" the entire word because one bit is often reserved as a *sign bit*: it indicates whether the number is positive or negative. In old computers, storage space was so scarce that "wasting" it in a sign seemed to be a shame in many cases where the number could never be negative. Thus, you will find old documentation and descriptions are integers and unsigned integers as separate types. Today, most integers on most operating systems do have a sign bit.

In describing the conversion of bits in a word to a binary number, there are two methods you can use. They are referred to as *big-endian* and *low-endian* depending on whether the sequence of bits should be interpreted from the most significant to least significant digit or vice versa.

This matters when you get down to the extreme details of architectures, but today this is generally hidden from view so that by the time you receive a stream of bits over a communications channel, the software at both ends has converted it to formats that don't rely on ended-ness.

Using Floating Point Numbers

There are a number of common ways of using floating point numbers. Typically, the implementation of floating point numbers is left to a special processor — a *floating point unit* (FPU). The basics of storing floating points numbers generally consist of the following logic:

- The number is basically stored as an integer that may be signed. This may be called a *significand*.

- Separately, an exponent is stored as another integer that also may be signed.

Together, most numbers can be represented. For example, the number 12 can be stored with a significand of 12 (base 10), which may be stored in binary as 1100.

BINARY NUMBER NOTATION

In common usage, we talk about the *places* of a number starting from the decimal point (see note later in this sidebar about decimal points) and moving to the left or the right. The first place to the left of the point is for values of 0 to the base - 1. In base-10, that means that place (or any other) can have the digits 0-9, but in base-2 any place can have digits 0-1.

The next place to the left is the base itself. Thus, in base-10, 12 is interpreted as 2x1 plus 1x10.

In binary, the number is 12. Start from the right-hand side, which is where the point would be and calculate:

0x1

0x2

1x4

1x8

The sum is 12.

The second place to the left is for the number of items in the base to the second power. Thus, in base-10, the number 213 is 3x1 plus 1x10, plus 2x100.

There is disagreement over what to call the decimal point in non-base-10 systems. Some people make the argument that a decimal point is unique to base-10 (decimal) systems. Others argue that it is not unique to base-10 just as *digit* can be used to refer to a character in any base as long as it is valid.

If you want an unambiguous generic term for the decimal point, you can call it a *radix point*. Mathematicians (and perhaps no one else) will understand you. In this chapter, we hedge a bit and refer to it as a *point*, which is a commonly used way of avoiding unnecessary arguments.

Storing Strings and Characters

Strings and characters are used to display text in apps … sometimes. Text can appear in images that are displayed in apps, and although you may think that they are strings and characters, when they are part of an image, they are as much an image as a photo of a cloud is.

Characters are represented by a sequence of bits. Depending on the characters and language involved, a different number of bits can be involved. Initially, characters in were six bits long, and then it stretched to eight. Today, with Unicode characters, most of the characters and most of the world's languages can be displayed. The most commonly used encodings you will encounter are UTF-8, UTF-16, and UTF-32 (the number represents the number of bits used in a single character.

Strings are sequences of characters. As you can see from the possible lengths of the characters, a string can easily extend far beyond a single computer word so strings are normally not stored on the stack but are accessed with some form of a reference word.

Creating New Types

When you declare a constant or variable, you specify its type. You can do that with a type annotation or by setting a value for the constant or variable so that Swift can infer the type as you see in the following examples.

```
var myVariable:Int  // type annotation
var myVariable = 20 // inferred type
```

The type annotation becomes important when the inferred type might be not what you want. For example, although 20 would let Swift infer an Int type, the following code will make the variable into a Double.

```
var myVariable: Double = 20 // type annotation overrides
inferred Int type
```

You can also declare new types in Swift. Other modern languages allow you to do this as well, but traditional languages limit the types you can use to what is built into the language and its compilers. This allows for the type checking described previously in this chapter to be used to catch errors at the coding/compiling process rather than when the user is trying to use your app.

You can declare new types in Swift. Once declared, you can use them just as the original types declaring variables and constants using them and using your new types in type annotations. Your new types are built on the existing types already in Swift (and in your own code). You can, for example, create a type that relies on Int types. Your type can be used alongside Int types. (You will see how this is useful in the following section, "Working with Tuples.")

To declare a new type, you use the Swift *typealias* syntax in which one type is aliased to another. One reason to do this is to improve the readability of your code. You can (and should) name your constants and variables in a way that makes it clear what they are, but sometimes you want to refine your nomenclature so that it is more precise. For example, if you as use the built-in String type to name items that you deal with in your app, using the String type is fine.

You may want to use a type alias to specify to yourself and others what exactly that string represents. So you could use a typealias like this:

```
typealias productName = String
```

You can now use productName in declarations such as the following

```
var widget1:productName = "Widget 1"
var widget2:productName = "Widget 2"
```

You can move beyond simple names to use a `typealias` for a collection type. For example, you could create an array of your inventory:

```
var inventory = Array <productName>()
inventory = [widget1, widget2]
```

You can add other arrays to an array as long as you respect the type. Because arrays can have duplicate elements, you can make another array out of `widget1` and add that array to inventory.

```
inventory += [widget1]
print (inventory)
```

You can see the results in Figure 7-1.

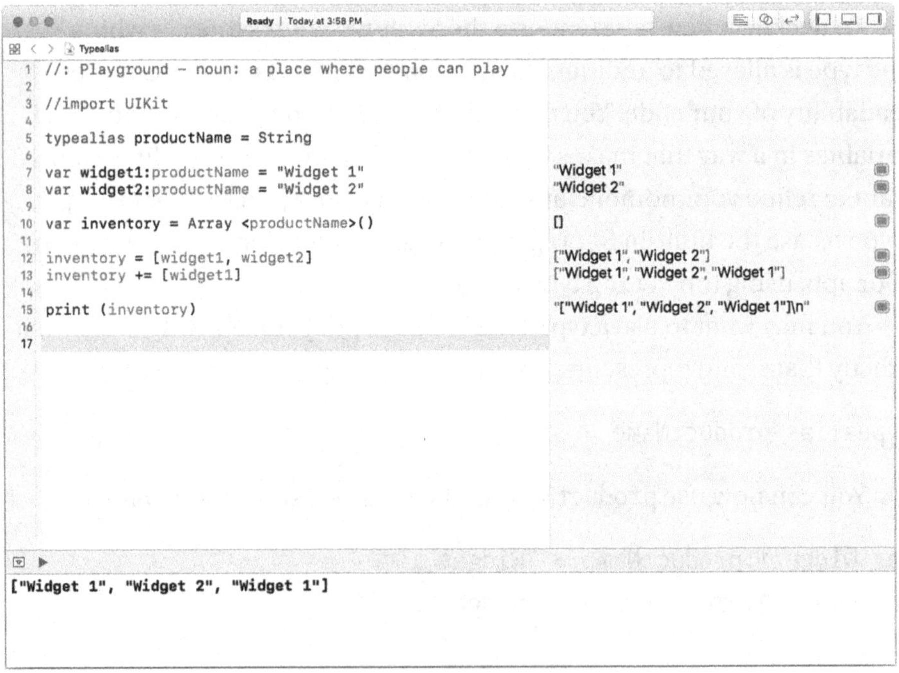

Figure 7-1. *Add another element to the array*

You can use the same logic to add a string in its own array to the inventory array.

```
inventory += ["dog"]
print (inventory)
```

You can add the string "dog" to inventory because inventory is an array of type productName that is a typealias for String.

If you apply the same logic to a new array of an Int (17), you'll get an error as you see in Figure 7-2. The array is an array of typealias productName (String) and so Int types are not allowed.

```
inventory += [17]
print (inventory)
```

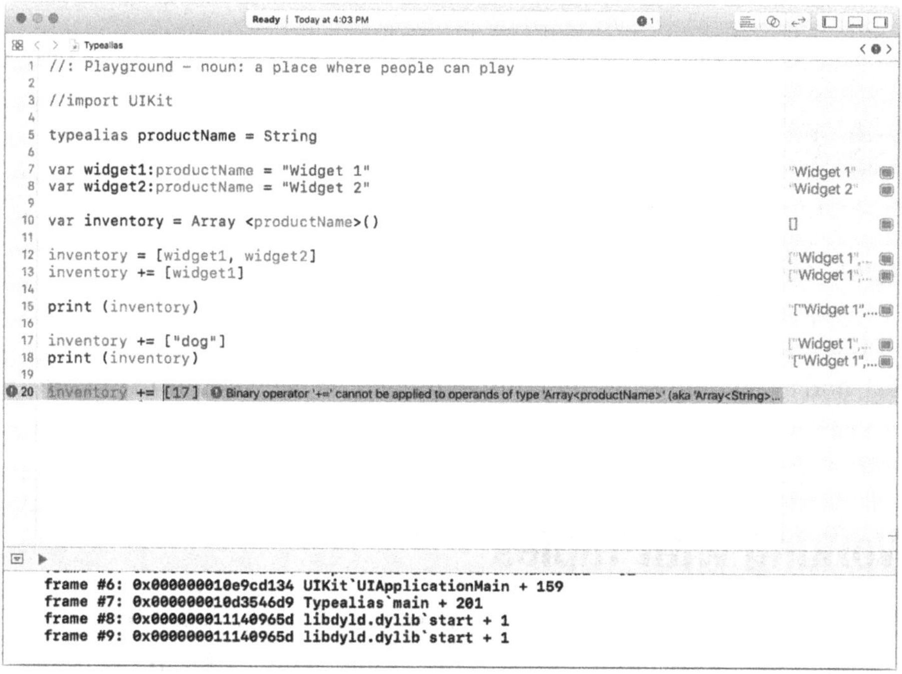

Figure 7-2. *You cannot add an Int to the array*

If you put the 17 in quotes so that it is a String, all will be well as you see in Figure 7-3.

```
//: Playground - noun: a place where people can play

//import UIKit

typealias productName = String

var widget1:productName = "Widget 1"                    "Widget 1"
var widget2:productName = "Widget 2"                    "Widget 2"

var inventory = Array <productName>()                   []

inventory = [widget1, widget2]                          ["Widget 1",...
inventory += [widget1]                                  ["Widget 1",...

print (inventory)                                       "["Widget 1",...

inventory += ["dog"]                                    ["Widget 1",...
print (inventory)                                       "["Widget 1",...

inventory += ["17"]                                     ["Widget 1",...
print (inventory)                                       "["Widget 1",...
```

```
["Widget 1", "Widget 2", "Widget 1"]
["Widget 1", "Widget 2", "Widget 1", "dog"]
["Widget 1", "Widget 2", "Widget 1", "dog", "17"]
```

Figure 7-3. *Add an Int as a String*

Using typealias to make your code more readable is a very useful idea, and it can help to prevent problems later on because the use of the type can be made clear to you and other people who maintain the code.

Working with Tuples

The numbers, strings, and characters described in the previous section are common to most computer languages today. There are variations that have been implemented over time in most languages, and Swift has many of them.

Skipping over the many variations on the basic number, string, and character types, we can look at a modern type that is implemented in Swift and other languages such as Python and C# in similar ways. A *tuple* is a sequence of types that together make up a single type.

You can, for instance, declare a tuple, which is a form of type that you create from other types. You use typealias to provide an alias to an existing type, and that existing type can be one that you create with a tuple. In fact, using typealias to name a tuple may be the most common use of typealias.

A tuple basically is a sequence of types enclosed in parentheses. It is used in a type annotation or alias. For example, you can create a tuple of two Double types to represent the dimensions (length and width) of a rectangle). You can give it a typealias of dimensions as in the following code:

```
typealias dimensions (Double, Double)
var myRectangle:dimensions = (2.0, 3.0)
```

You don't have to use a typealias. You can create and use a tuple very simple as in the following code:

```
var myRectangle = (2.0, 3.0)
```

There is no need to name a tuple type with a typealias unless you want to refer to it elsewhere.

Tuples can be incredibly useful because they combine several items in one addressable symbol (the typealias name if there is one). A function in most languages can return a result that is normally one item. Many people let a function return a collection (array, dictionary, or set), which has the effect of returning multiple results. (In fact, dictionaries have commonly been used to return multiple results in a single item.)

The items in a tuple are identified by order: You can't rearrange them. By default they are numbered starting at zero. Figure 7-4 shows how you can create and use tuples. Notice in the viewer that follows line three that the two elements of the tuple are shown preceded by their default names — .0 and .1. .

When declaring a tuple, you can provide names for the items. In Figure 7-4, note that in line 7 the items are named:

```
typealias dimensionsLabeled = (width: Double, height: Double)
```

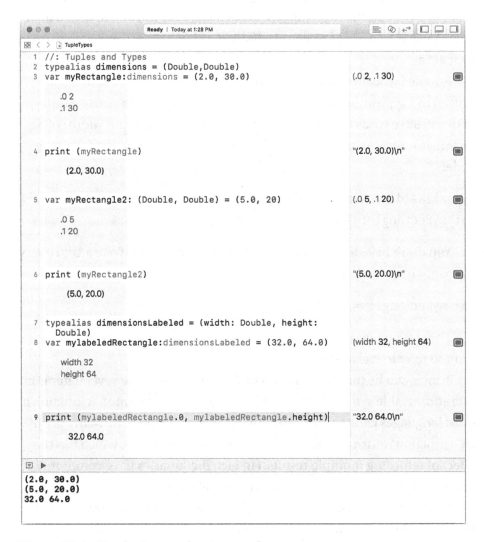

Figure 7-4. *Declaring and using tuples*

You can refer to the items in a tuple by using the name of the variable or constant followed by dot syntax and the name of each item as in line 9:

```
print (myLabeledRectangle.0, myLabeledRectangle.height)
```

Even if you provide a name for an item in a tuple, you can still refer to it by its default number.

Note   The names of tuple elements are not quoted strings.

Summary

This chapter provides you with an overview of types as used for data. You see the types that are common to all languages and operating systems (numbers, characters, and strings) as well as types that you can create such as tuples.

The use of types — even dynamic types — can make your code safer to develop and to maintain.

With the data side of things under control, it is time to move on to look at how operating systems and applications actually work with the data that you declare and store. That is the topic of the next chapter.

CHAPTER 8

Managing Control Flow: Conditionals, Switches, and Enumerations

In Chapter 5, you saw the basics of repetitions, but there's a lot more to managing control flow than looping through repetition code. This chapter explores the other main control flow aspects of code. These are present in most languages and operating systems.

What's Next?

The basic flow of control in an app is from one line of code to the next. A single line of code is a single statement even though it may involve many steps — perhaps this is because the line of code causes a function or method to run. Furthermore, several lines of code can be placed on one physical line of code in Swift. As in many other languages a semicolon is placed after each line of code when more than one is placed on a single

143

© Jesse Feiler 2018
J. Feiler, *Learn Computer Science with Swift*, https://doi.org/10.1007/978-1-4842-3066-4_8

line. Furthermore, to improve readability, a single line of code can be stretched over several physical lines of code. Nevertheless, we refer to a "line of code" as if it were both a physical and logical entity even though there is not an exact equivalence.

No matter how it is formatted, each line of code is executed in an app, and, most of the time, after it is completed, the next line of code is executed. If there are no more lines of code, the app terminates.

This is the basic pattern for apps and programs from the dawn of computer time. It is important to note that there is a major variation on this pattern that is particularly prevalent in apps that rely on user interaction. In these cases, the app starts running, and, once it has started running, it waits for an external event to be passed to it (that event might be a user action). When the event is received, the app processes it and then waits for its next event. A program like this may terminate only when the computer is turned off or restarted.

On iOS devices, you can specifically terminate apps that are waiting for events. You can see them in Control Center as you see in Figure 8-1. Just drag an app up to the top of the window to terminate it.

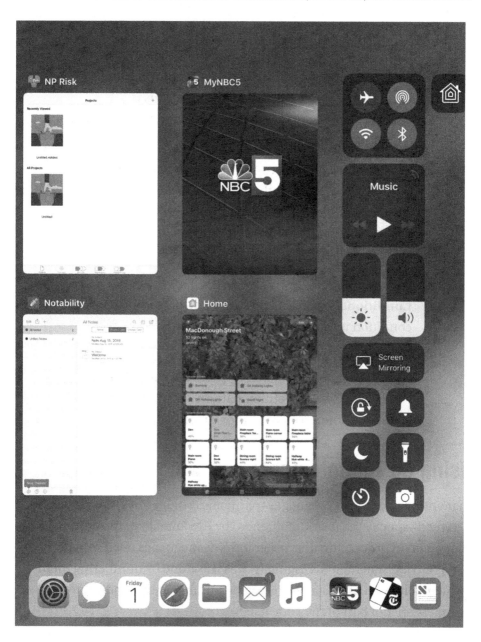

Figure 8-1. *See running apps in Control Center on iOS 11 and later*

Within an app, the major exceptions to the next-line-of-code sequence are the following:

- **Go to**. You can explicitly go to another line of code other than the next line. As you will see, this is normally discouraged, but it remains a commonly used technique of managing control.

- **Switch**. You can execute one of several lines of code (or sections of code) rather than the next line. This is a useful technique to use when you want to do one of several operations (show the current temperature, show the calendar for next week, log out, or anything else).

- **Conditionals**. You can execute a line of code if some condition is (or isn't) true.

- **Repetitions**. You can repeat one or more lines of code as you saw in Chapter 5. There are a number of variations on the repetition pattern — you can repeat code until some condition is or isn't true, for example.

Using Go To Statements...Or Not

In many programming languages (particularly older ones) it is possible to directly specify the next statement to be executed after the current statement. In order to do this, programming languages need some way of identifying statements. Originally, this was done by numbering them sequentially. Statements in Swift may be numbered by Xcode, but the numbers are not part of the code itself.

In some languages (notably PL/1 and COBOL), statements can be named. This is better than numbering them because the names don't change if you insert or delete statements. Line numbers are fragile. When labels are used, they often must be the first characters on a line if they are used on that line, and the label is terminated by a period, colon, or other distinctive character. They typically cannot contain embedded blanks.

In Swift and most modern languages, even if line numbers are shown, they are only for your reference: you cannot transfer control to a specific line number.

Figure 8-2 shows a Swift playground in Xcode with line numbers shown.

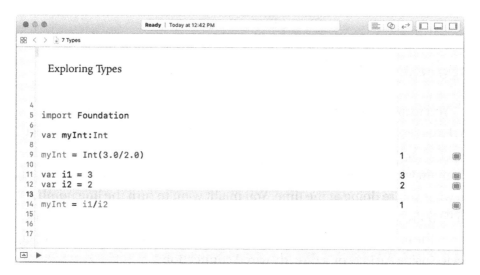

Figure 8-2. *Swift playground with lines numbers shown*

Figure 8-3 shows the same code with line numbers hidden.

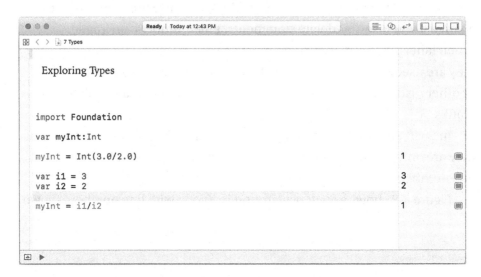

Figure 8-3. *Swift playground with line numbers hidden*

You turn line numbers on and off in Xcode preferences (Xcode ➤ Preferences) as shown in Figure 8-4. Once Preferences has opened, select Text Editing from the top bar and choose the Editing option at the top of the main window section. You can turn line numbers on and off depending on what you're doing at the time. You might want to turn the line numbers on if you're going to a code review meeting where people will want to talk about the code whether it is printed out or shown on an Apple TV or other device using AirPlay or a directly wired connection.

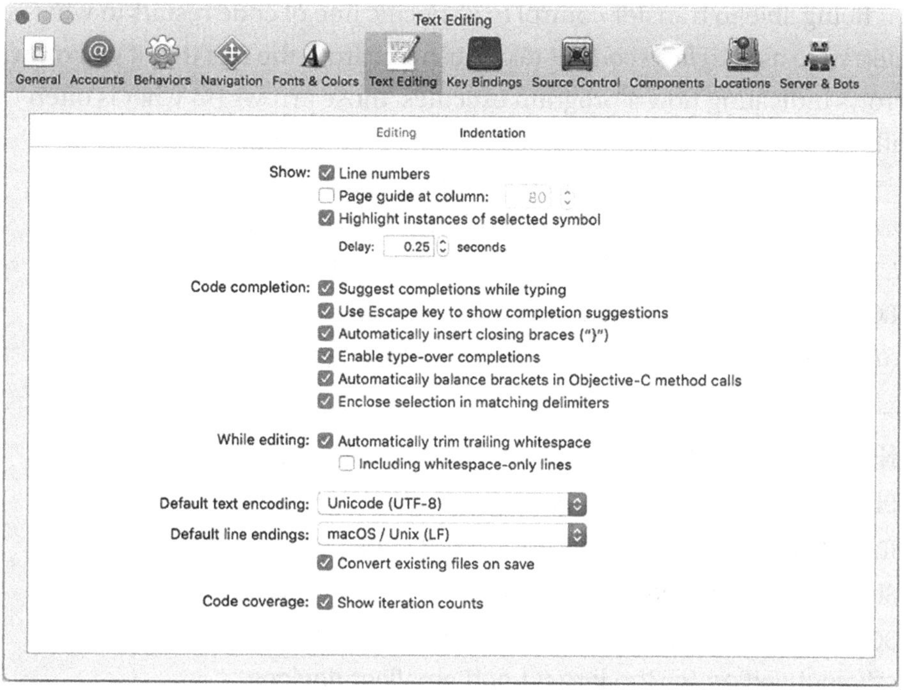

Figure 8-4. *Xcode line number preferences in Xcode preferences*

Line numbers along with go to statements have become artifacts of the past in the coding world, but, just as in the physical world, the past is always with us or, as William Faulkner wrote, "The past is never dead. It's not even past." [*Requiem for a Nun* and various misquoted variations on the web] Being able to identify line numbers in discussions and documents is very useful. (Line numbers are frequently used in the screenshots from Xcode in this book, for example.)

Being able to specify a specific line as the next line to execute has proven to be a dangerous programming technique. If you are writing code and thinking about finding a way to jump to something other than the next line of code, use one of the other techniques that are described in this section.

Being able to transfer control to a specific line of code results in what is referred to as *spaghetti code*. It takes its name from the fact that if you draw arrows indicating how a program executes, those arrows (in what is often called a *flow chart*) start to look like a plate of spaghetti.

The alternative to line numbers and spaghetti code is *structured programming* or *structured code*. The term was devised by Edsger W. Dijkstra in 1968. A leading developer on the Burroughs Corporation ALGOL programming team, his influence on that project and computer programming in general in the late 1950s was enormous.

Note   ALGOL on Burroughs mainframes was my second programming language (my first was FORTRAN on CDC 6600 mainframes, which in the 1960s were considered the first successful supercomputer). Much of the ALGOL syntax is relevant today and some of its features are hallmarks of good programming style and efficient coding for the largest and smallest devices.

Rather than transferring control to a specific line identified by label or number, structured programming relies on structuring in the code into logical sections (functions, procedures, or methods that you will find out more about in Chapter 10, "Building Components,"). You can then transfer control to the logical section, which may contain multiple lines of code. Because of this structure, you don't transfer control all over your code from one line to another to another and so on (thus, the origin of the phrase *spaghetti code*).

Using Conditionals

Perhaps the simplest way of structuring your code to avoid random jumping around from one statement to some other statement and then on to confusion is to set up a binary choice. If some condition is true, then execute the following line of code. This means that instead of jumping around, you simply do or don't execute the next line of code. The structure and flow of your code remains fairly easy to understand.

You can even begin to expand on this pattern by setting up a three-way choice: if a condition is true, execute this line of code, and if it is not true, execute that line of code. Note that these are not distant lines of code — they are sequential. In this way, the choice is easy to understand and the flow of control is simple.

You can build even more by using compound statements so that a group of statements are treated as one. The logic is then modified a little so that conceptually it is

If this condition is true execute these following lines of code;
if it is not true execute those lines of code.

The lines of code remain sequential so that the condition (or if statement) is evaluated and several lines that follow it are executed or, if the condition is not true, several other lines that follow are executed. Although the control takes one set of statements rather than another, all of the code is together.

The initial part of this pattern is the conditional expression itself. In its simplest form, it is an if statement. The basic style in Swift (and many other languages) is illustrated in this code snippet:

Listing 8-1. Using a Swift if statement

```
var x = 5

if x > 4
{
  x = x + 1
}
```

In languages in the C family, the syntax is slightly different, as shown in Listing 8-2:

Listing 8-2. Using a C if statement

```
if (x > 4)
  x = x + 1;
```

As you can see, it is necessary to somehow differentiate between the conditional test and the code to be executed (or not executed). Parentheses or brackets are used for these purposes.

These are the concepts. Specific Swift examples follow.

Using Compound Statements in Swift

In many languages (including Swift) you can group statements together by enclosing them in brackets as in the following:

```
{
  let x = 5
  let y = 6
}
```

This lets you treat the statements as a compound statement — that is, one statement. This is particularly useful when used in conjunction with a conditional test. This means that the Swift example shown previously in Listing 8-1 can be enhanced. The brackets around the conditional code mean that it is already a compound statement. To make the if statement apply to several statements within a compound statement, you just add the second statement to the interior of the bracketed compound statement as in Listing 8-3.

Listing 8-3. Using a Swift if statement with a compound statement

```
var x = 5

if x > 4
{
  x = x + 1
  print ("updated x")
}
```

You can use Xcode's preferences to manage indentation. Choose Xcode ➤ Preferences and select Text Editing and the Indentation segment at the top of the pane as shown in Figure 8-5.

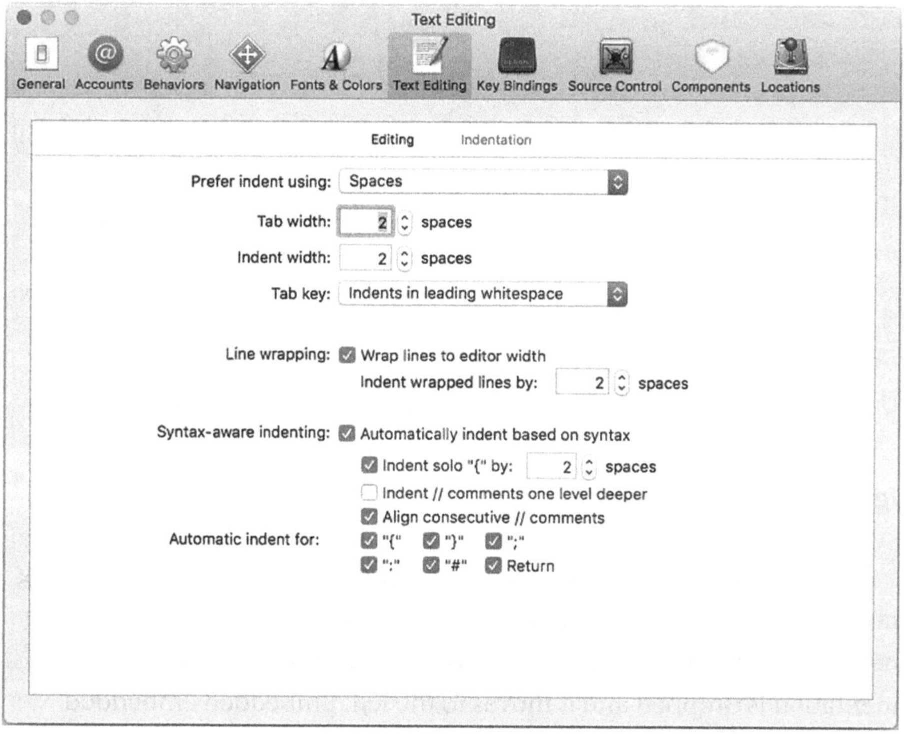

Figure 8-5. *Setting indentation options*

With the settings shown in Figure 8-5, you can see how indentation works in Figure 8-6. (The error is due to the fact that a disembodied compound statement such as this one that is used only for a formatting demonstration isn't valid syntax.)

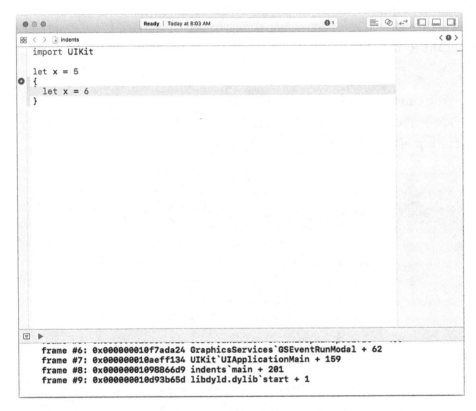

```
import UIKit

let x = 5
{
    let x = 6
}
```

```
frame #6: 0x000000010f7ada24 GraphicsServices`GSEventRunModal + 62
frame #7: 0x000000010aeff134 UIKit`UIApplicationMain + 159
frame #8: 0x00000001098866d9 indents`main + 201
frame #9: 0x000000010d93b65d libdyld.dylib`start + 1
```

Figure 8-6. *Using indentation in Xcode preferences*

What you don't see in Figure 8-6 is that after typing the initial opening bracket, the insertion point moves to the indented space on the following line so you can keep typing. When you type the closing bracket, the indentation is dropped and it moves to the left. Embedded embedded statements of any length display properly.

Note that there are different styles and standards for indenting code. One of the most basic is where to place the opening bracket. This is particularly important in conditional statements where there is code before the opening bracket of a compound statement. The two basic styles are shown in Listing 8-4 and Listing 8-5.

Listing 8-4. Dangling bracket

```
if x > 4
{
  x = x + 1
  print ("updated x")
}
```

Listing 8-5. Embedded bracket

```
if x > 4 {
  x = x + 1
  print ("updated x")
}
```

There are arguments to be made for both styles. In the dangling style, the opening and closing brackets are aligned so it may be easier to pick out the compound statement. In the embedded style (Listing 8-5), the opening and closing brackets are not aligned, but the entire conditional statement appears as one unit (which it is).

The issue can be a bit more complicated when you expand an `if` statement to provide an `else` clause — that is, a statement or compound statement to be executed if the condition is false. Listing 8-6 shows one version of a dangling `else` bracket. Common variations on this style do not indent the `else`.

Listing 8-6. Dangling else bracket

```
if x > 4
{
  x = x + 1
  print ("updated x")
}
  else
{
  print ("no update")
}
```

In Listing 8-7, you see an embedded else. By comparison with Listing 8-6, this emphasizes the two components of the if statement. Which style you use is a matter of preference (your preference and the preferences of your project team).

Listing 8-7. Embedded else bracket

```
if x > 4 {
  x = x + 1
  print ("updated x")
} else {
  print ("no update")
}
```

Ternary Operators

So far in this chapter, the discussion has focused on the control of statements within an app. There is a related operator that is used in a somewhat similar way. *The ternary operator* does not manage control flow; rather, within a single statement it lets you choose between two alternate values as a result. It is discussed here because it frequently is used to replace more complex if statements.

The situation that ternary operators address is a common if pattern:

```
if x > 10 {
  message = "greater than 10"
} else {
  message = "not greater than 10"
}
```

Whether the condition is true or false, the message will be set to something. With a ternary operator, you can make this much simpler. The code using a ternary operator is a single line of code:

```
message = x > 10 ? "greater than 10" : "not greater than 10"
```

This is a replacement statement that incorporates the conditional test and both the true and false results. Figure 8-7 shows this in a playground.

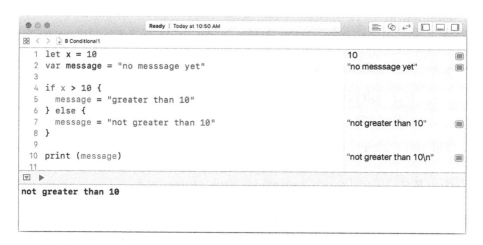

Figure 8-7. *Explore a ternary operator*

You can test this code for yourself by downloading the Conditional1 playground as described in the Introduction. Try adjusting the value of x in the first line of code and the test for x > 10 in the ternary operator; you can also experiment with changing the text strings.

Remember that ternary operators are operators within a single statement (not even a compound statement although you can get fancy and produce some almost undecipherable code if you try to push that limit).

Switching Control

Conditional statements let you branch to one of two true/false conditions; you can also place conditional statements within one or more branches so that you continue to fork along true/false paths of various conditions. If you want to implement more than a simple binary true/false branch, you may find yourself deep in confusing branches of branches. You may realize that what you want is more than two choices, but the `if` statement limits you to one or two choices (two choices require an `else` clause as part of the `if` statement).

The abstract idea of a switch statement is as follows:

- A condition is evaluated.

- Its result is used to choose a statement or set of statements to be executed.

The basic idea is shown here in pseudocode in Listing 8-8:

Listing 8-8. Pseudocode generic switch statement

```
switch <expression to evaluate> {
  case <expressionResult1>: <one or more statements to execute>
  case <expressionResult2>: <another one or more statements to
  execute>
}
```

Comparing Swift Switches to Other Languages

Note that the entire `switch` statement is enclosed in delimiters (brackets in this case). `Switch` statements are great tools for writing structured code, but there are a number of significant variations across languages. Here are some of them:

- Once an expression is evaluated and matched to an expression result, that code is executed, but what happens next? In some languages such as C, after `expressionResult1` is chosen and executed, control will pass to the following statements. The word `break` is used at the end of a `case` element to cause control to simply leave the entire `switch` statement.

- `break` statements can appear anywhere. If you have five `case` elements, you can place a `break` command after any of them. You could choose the first `case` element, execute it, drop through to execute the second `case` element, and then terminate if a `break` statement is at the end of the second `case` element.

- In languages in the ALGOL and Pascal families (including Swift), the choice is limited to executing the `case` element. There may not be a need for a `break` statement. (This is the case in Swift.)

- The entire statement may be called a `switch`, a `case`, or `select`.

- The `case` elements are often called cases and are identified by the keyword `case`.

- Some languages (including Swift) let you modify the conditions under which a `case` element is chosen.

- Many languages require a special case (often called default), which is executed if there is no case element matching the expression result.

Much of the variations may be due to the fact that although the statement is powerful and can help you create more structured and readable code, developers added additional features rapidly, and they were inconsistent. This may have been related to the period in which these statements were developed — it was a time (the 1960s) of a great deal of language development and modification.

Exploring the Swift Switch Syntax

The Swift switch statement is highly structured and powerful. If you are familiar with other language switch statements, it may be new to you, so the basic Swift syntax is provided here and will continue in the "Using Enumerations" section that follows).

The basic Swift syntax is shown in Listing 8-9. It is the same as the generic pseudocode in Listing 8-8 but it has a default statement. The default statement is required in Swift, and its interpretation may be different than it is in other languages you are used to.

Swift switch statements must be *exhaustive*. That means that if the controlling expression is of a certain type, the default statement applies to all elements of that type other than those identified in case statements.

Listing 8-9. Basic Swift switch statement

```
switch <expression to evaluate> {
  case <expressionResult1>: <one or more statements to execute>
  case <expressionResult2>: <another one or more statements to
  execute>
  default: <one or more statements to execute>
}
```

This means that the controlling expression must have a type (and all expressions have a type either implicitly or explicitly). `break` statements are not required in Swift: a `case` expression executes and is terminated by the next `case` element or by the end of the `switch` statement.

You can have multiple values handled by a single case element in Swift. You simply combine the case elements as in:

```
case "result1", "result2":
```

In some other languages, you might be used to writing it differently; this code won't work in Swift because control doesn't pass from one case element to the next. It is terminated by the next `case` element.

```
case "result1":
case "result2":
```

You can also use a number of other conditions for case elements. Two are described in the following sections.

Using Advanced Switch Case Elements: Ranges

Listing 8-10 shows the use of a Swift switch using a range. The code begins with the declaration of an optional variable (myUserID), which is an `Int`.

It is set to 6 so it has a value, but note that if it is not set (that is an unset optional) this code will still function properly and not cause an error. It uses optional binding to set userID (if possible) to the unwrapped value of myUserID.

Note   There is more on optionals and optional binding in Chapter 9.

The switch statement now uses userID (the unwrapped value of myUserID) to choose a case statement to execute. In this case, the case is defined using a Swift range:

```
5..<9
```

This Swift syntax means the range between 5 and 9. Note that there are three characters in the range: 2 periods followed by <. It is not three characters followed by <.

Listing 8-10. A Swift switch with a range

```
var myUserID:Int?

myUserID = 6

if let userID = myUserID {
  switch (userID) {
  case 5..<9: print ("first example:" + String(userID))
  default: print ("not a known ID")
  }
}
```

You can see the code in action in Figure 8-8.

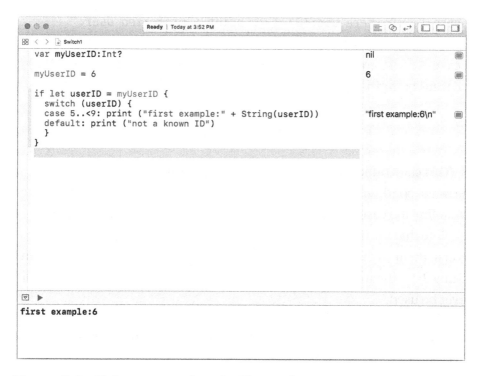

Figure 8-8. *Using a range in a Swift switch*

Using Advanced Switch Case Elements: Where Clauses

You can also create compound conditions with where in the case element, as in the code shown in Listing 8-11.

Listing 8-11. Using a where clause in a Swift switch

```
var myUserID:Int?

myUserID = 6

if let userID2 = myUserID {
  switch (userID2) {
```

```
    case 5..<9 where userID2 < 7: print ("preferred user:" +
    String(userID2))
    case 5..<9: print ("not a preferred user:" + String(userID2))
    default: print ("not a known ID")

    }
}
```

This code builds on the code shown previously in Listing 8-10. Here, the range condition is used twice. The first time, a where clause is added to it to refine the case condition. The second time there is no where clause.

Note that these cases are evaluated one at a time in sequence. If you reverse them so that the where follows the unconditional case as shown in Listing 8-12, the unconditional case will be used and the where clause will never be used.

Listing 8-12. Reversing where and general cases in a switch statement

```
if let userID2 = myUserID {
  switch (userID2) {
  case 5..<9: print ("not a preferred user:" + String(userID2))
  case 5..<9 where userID2 < 7: print ("preferred user:" +
  String(userID2))
  default: print ("not a known ID")

  }
}
```

This code is shown executing in Figure 8-9.

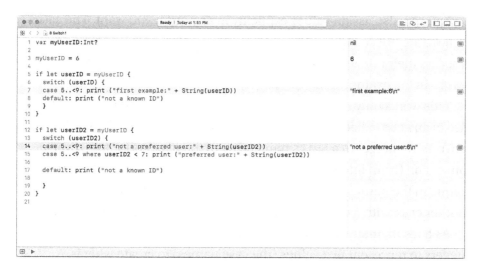

Figure 8-9. *Using a where clause in a Swift switch*

Using Enumerated Types

Just as Swift switch statements build on existing switch statements in many languages, so, too, Swift enumerations (*enums*) build on enumerations in other languages. Enumerated types (shortened to *enums* in common usage) are just that: a type that is constructed by enumerating its values.

The most common example of an enumerated type is *Suit*, which has the values *Clubs, Spades, Hearts,* and *Diamonds*. In many program languages (particularly the C languages), the order of enumerated types matters because an integer number can be inferred or assigned to each type value. Thus, in the example of *Clubs, Spades, Hearts,* and *Diamonds*, the values by default would be as follows:

```
Clubs = 0
Spades = 1
Hearts = 2
Diamonds = 3
```

You can also assign values explicitly in any order you want. The cases of enums are not strings so they are not quoted. You can use enum cases to access their integer values. This means that you can use the enum case Hearts in the example above as 2.

This works only in one direction: you can't use 2 to indicate the Hearts case of an enum called Suits. You can, however, write a small function that converts an integer to a Suits name. One of the reasons for this reverse conversion (from integer to enum case name) is that enum integers are not unique in the namespace: the enum case Spades can have a value of 1 and another enum with case Flowers can use the value of 1 for Geraniums.

As a result, many people think of enums primarily as ways to use integers to represent text values (the case names) to create what is sometimes referred to as self-documenting code. (Some other people refer to this as a joke. It's an area of contention.)

Swift's Approach to Enumerated Types

Swift has turned enumerated types into first-class types rather than just a typing or documentation shortcut. In Swift the case names are (as in other languages) not quoted strings. The notion of automatically assigning values is used in some cases, but you can assign a raw value to each case. That raw value can be an integer (as in most languages), but it can also be a string, character, or number — even a floating point number).

Swift enums style capitalizes the enum name and uses lowercase for the case values as in the following declarations.

```
enum Suit {
  case club
  case spade
  case heart
  case diamond
}
```

Using Swift Enums with Switch Statements

Because enums in Swift are more tightly structured than in many other languages, they fit well into Swift features such as the requirement that switch statement case elements be exhaustive. You can use an enum to assign a value as in the following line of code that assigns the enum case club of the Suit enum to a constant called cardSuit:

```
let cardSuit = Suit.club
```

You can then start to create a switch statement that uses cardSuit. If you attempt to close the switch statement, you will get an error as shown in Figure 8-10.

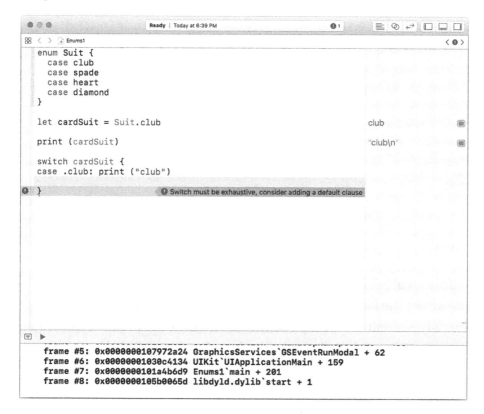

Figure 8-10. *Swift flags non-exhaustive switch statements*

167

This error message is made possible because Swift keeps track of the cases for each enum. If you heed the message and type in the other cases, you will no longer have an error as you see in Figure 8-11.

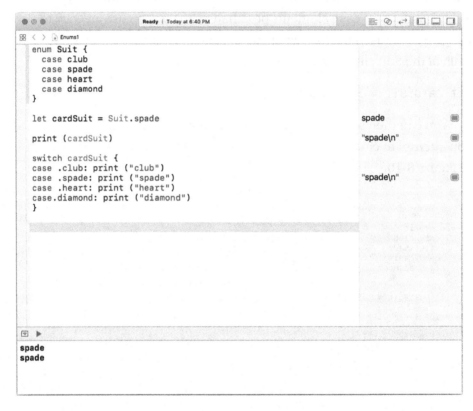

Figure 8-11. *Creating an exhaustive switch statement with an enum*

Instead of printing out a message for each case of a switch statement, you can use the fact that enums are full-fledged types to refer to them more generally, instead of printing out what the name of the case element is as you see in Figure 8-11 or in Listing 8-13.

Listing 8-13. Simplifying the switch statement.

```
switch cardSuit {
default: print (cardSuit)
}
```

In Listing 8-13 all of the control flows through the default case, and you don't even need the switch at all. You can achieve the same result with one line of code:

```
print (cardSuit)
```

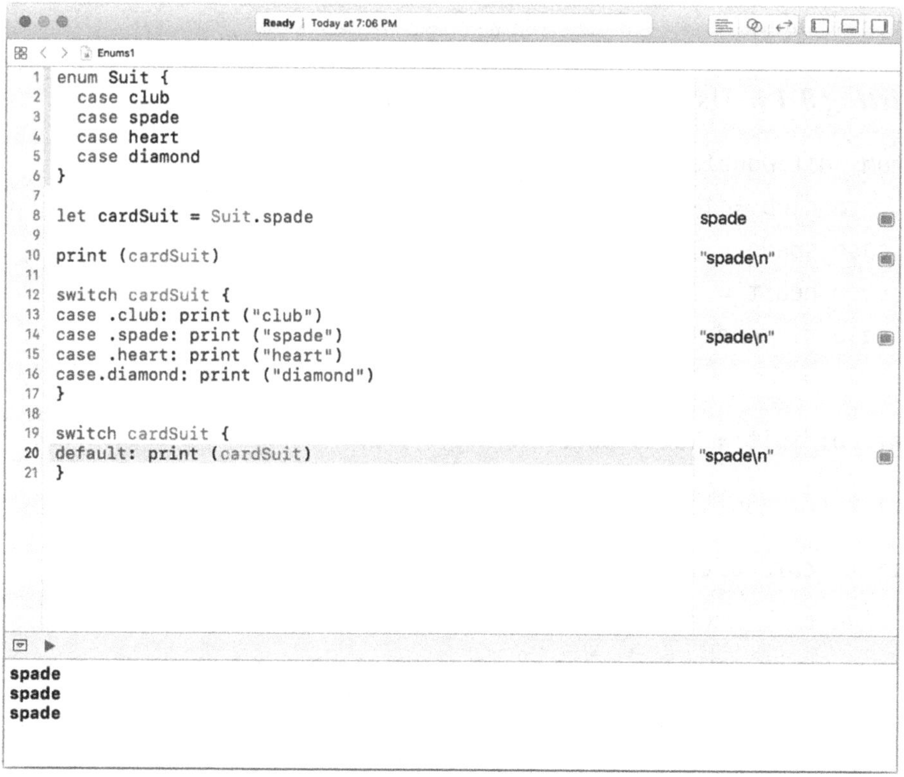

Figure 8-12.

You can set the raw value of an enum. As noted previously, the raw value can be a number (integer or floating point), character, string, or other value. You simply add it in the enum declaration as shown in Listing 8-14.

If you do that, you can then retrieve it by accessing the rawValue property of an enum as in

cardSuit.rawValue

The example shown previously in this chapter is updated in Figure 8-13 to show how you can print the raw value. You can access the raw value for any purpose — it doesn't have to be for printing. You can use a numeric value to perform calculations, and you can also add a meaningful string to the case name.

Listing 8-14. Using raw values in an enum

```
enum Suit:Double {
    case club = 15.3
    case spade = 32.6
    case heart = 0.0
    case diamond = -42.3
}

let cardSuit = Suit.spade

print (cardSuit)

print (cardSuit.rawValue)
```

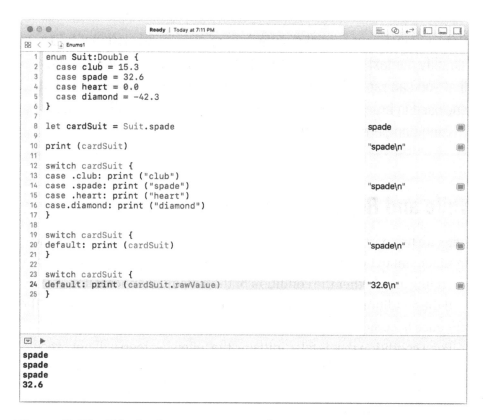

Figure 8-13. *Displaying enum raw values*

Exploring Repetitions and Strides

Most programming languages support a variety of repetition operators.
You see the basics in Chapter 5, "Managing Control Flow: Repetition" but
here is an overview of the common repetition variations. (All are available
in Swift, and, with occasional modifications, in most other languages you
may use.)

There are two basic types of repetition loops: while loops and for
loops. All repeat a statement or compound statement. while loops rely
on conditional statements for their control but for loops rely on data
structures for their control.

Note   Repetitions repeat a statement or compound statement. To simplify the text, this section refers to statements, but rest assured that you can replace a single statement with a compound statement enclosed in brackets { } as was discussed previously in this chapter ("Using Compound Statements").

While and Repeat-While Loops

There are two parts to a while loop: the condition that is true or false and the statement to be repeated. The while loop behaves slightly differently depending on whether the condition or the statement appears first.

If the condition is false when the while statement begins execution, the difference becomes clear.

For a condition that is false initially, the following loop will not execute. The code is executed as it would be in a natural language. Because the while condition isn't true, it won't execute. When the condition becomes false, the while loop terminates.

Note   If the condition never becomes false, the loop becomes an infinite loop and will never stop. If the logic of your app is such that the condition doesn't change, you don't want a while loop: You want an if statement.

```
while <condition> {
    <statement>
}
```

The other version of the while statement always executes at least once. Here is the basic code:

```
repeat {
  <statement>
} while <condition>
```

This loop will always execute at least once.

For-in Loops

These repetitions rely on collections (arrays, dictionaries, or sets). The main for-in loops rely on iterations and enumerations.

Iterating Over a Collection

The simplest version simply loops through the collection (this is called *iteration*). Listing 8-15 shows three simple collections (an array, a dictionary, and a set) and how you can loop through each one with the same syntax.

Listing 8-15. Using for-in loops for collections

```
let myArray = ["dog", 4.6] as [Any]
let myDictionary = ["name": "Rover", "weight": 20.5] as
[String : Any]
let mySet = ["name", "weight"]

for arrayItem in myArray {
  print (arrayItem)
}

for dictionaryItem in myDictionary {
  print (dictionaryItem)
}
```

```
for setElement in mySet {
  print (setElement)
}
```

You can see this in the playground shown in Figure 8-14.

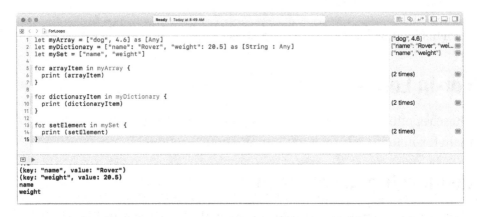

Figure 8-14. *Explore loops in a playground*

It is very common that you just want to deal with each item in a collection in turn, and this does that job.

Looping Through Indexes (Arrays) and Keys (Dictionaries)

In the case of arrays and dictionaries, sometimes you need not only the value of the item but its index (in an array) and its key (in a dictionary).

Note   Because sets are unordered, there are no keys or indexes to use, so all you can do is iterate through the set elements as described in the previous section.

There is a difference between iterating over elements of a collection as described in the previous section and enumerating those elements. You will see that in this section where an array is enumerated. That enumeration provides each element of the array along with its index. (Remember that array indexes are part of the array structure itself and not part of the data.)

The built-in enumerated function provides tuples for each element of the array. Each tuple consists of the array index and the value. If you call enumerated() on an array, you will see those tuples as shown in Figure 8-15. Note that the data used previously has been changed to include a third item (cat) in the array. The data viewer in the playground shows the array with its three elements. If you open it with the disclosure triangle, you'll see the three indexes and their associated values.

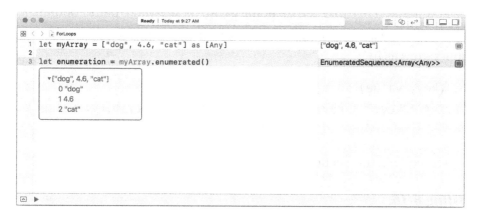

Figure 8-15. *Results of enumerated() on an array*

If you want to use the enumerated values, you can display them with code such as the following. First, the enumerated function is called on the myArray array. Then, a for-in loop operates on the myArray.enumerated() result. The two values in each tuple are printed out.

175

```
for (index, item) in myArray.enumerated() {
  print ("index: " + String(index) + " item:" +
  String(describing: item))
}
```

The tuple names that you use don't matter because it's the order of the items in the tuple that matter. If you want to change the code like this, it will still work as well (as long as you update the print statement to match the names you're giving to the tuple values.

It is important to note that because you are dealing with values that are not all strings, you can take the Fix-It suggestions you'll get in Xcode to convert the numbers to strings. They rely on the String(describing:) function as you see in the code in this section.

To do a comparable enumeration with a dictionary, you don't need to call enumerated because the dictionary with its key-value pairs contains the keys as well as the values with its data. Thus, you can just name the tuple values as in

```
for (key, value) in myDictionary {
  print ("key:" + key + " value:" + String(describing: value))
}
```

The code in this section is shown in Listing 8-16.

Listing 8-16.

```
let myArray = ["dog", 4.6] as [Any]
let myDictionary = ["name": "Rover", "weight": 20.5] as
[String : Any]

for (index, item) in myArray.enumerated() {
  print ("index: " + String(index) + " item:" +
  String(describing: item))
}
```

```
for (key, value) in myDictionary {
  print ("key:" + key + " value:" + String(describing: value))
}
```

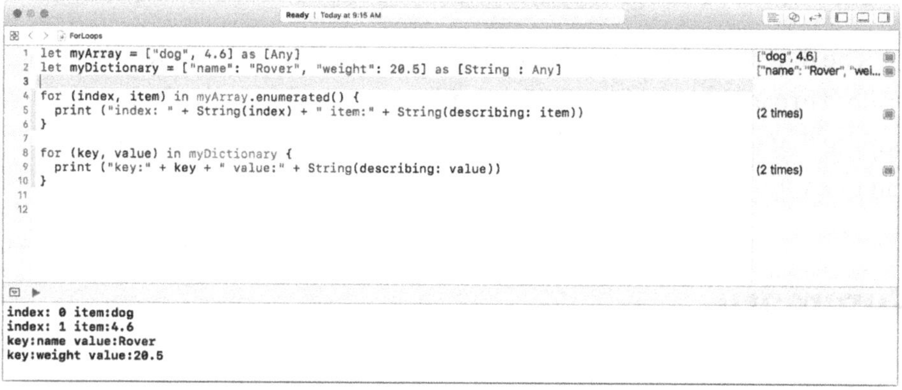

Figure 8-16. *Showing keys and indexes for dictionaries and arrays*

Using Strides

In addition to the built-in repetitions (for-in and while), the Swift Standard Library includes several that are frequently used in these situations. You have already seen the enumerated() function, and it is worth exploring others. One Standard Library function you may find useful is the stride(from:to:by:) function. This function can be adopted by types that adopt the Strideable protocol. You don't have to worry much about what that entails: just remember the list of types that are Strideable:

CGFloat
Decimal
Double
Float
Float80

177

When dealing with arrays of those types, you can apply the two `stride` functions:

```
stride (from: to: by:)
stride (from: through: by:)
```

The difference between them is whether the limit is included in the stride (`through`) or not (`to`). With `stride`, you can do some of the C-style looping that you may be used to (specifically, you can look not just from and to a value but using steps rather than increments of one.

Summary

This chapter goes into some basic computer science principles that are common to many languages. In two of the topics discussed (enumerations and switch statements), you see how Swift extends common functionality and also makes common features more rigorously defined and used.

Having looked at data and types as well as control flow, you have many of the basics of computer science at hand. The next step is to move on to storing and retrieving data. After all, without those features, users have to start from scratch each time they run an app.

CHAPTER 9

Storing Data and Sharing Data

Computer science focuses on the design and use of computers in one standard phrase. Although there are early examples of computer-like devices (notably the Charles Babbage Analytical Engine in the 1830s, the Jacquard loom in 1804, and the Enigma machines in the 1930s and through the Second World War with Turing's advances), the modern computer age really began in the 1940s. The big steps forward in the 1940s were significant hardware advances, and, arguably, the most important step forward was the development of programming and compilers so that computers could generate their own instructions from English-like code written by humans. (Look at information about Grace Hopper and her colleagues on the Internet for more details of the software side of things.)

Even with the development of personal computers in the late 1970s and the rise of the Internet in the 1990s, not much changed in the basics of computer science as new technologies and new capabilities emerged. One thing that has changed — quite dramatically — is the storing and sharing of data.

Whereas the advances in computer hardware have often been dramatically heralded in the media, changes related to data seem to be of less interest to many people. In fact, many people consider data and data

179

© Jesse Feiler 2018
J. Feiler, *Learn Computer Science with Swift*, https://doi.org/10.1007/978-1-4842-3066-4_9

management to be an almost trivial part of the computer science world. Oh, yes, there's data, and it needs to be stored somewhere, but let's look at exciting things like 3D printing, social media, and forget about that mundane data storage. (Ask almost any data management specialist for an opinion on this topic, and you're likely to unleash a veritable torrent of comments on the matter.)

The role of data is critical to computer science and its applications, and that role has evolved in ways that few people have focused on until very recently. This chapter addresses the data issues in computer science. It is divided into four sections that address the four primary data concerns:

- **What is the data?** All apps generate, consume, and store data. You may think your app is the exception, but there are no exceptions if you look at all the data that your app generates, consumes, and stores.

- **Where is the data stored?** With the exception of data that is generated by hardware and software on demand, the data that makes apps possible needs to be stored somewhere. Sometimes the app is creating data, and if that is the case, it typically needs to be stored somewhere even if that location is temporary and on some scratchpad that is built into the system or the app.

- **Who is in charge of the data?** Is it static or is it updated periodically (and, if it is updated, who does that)? Who owns the data (that's not an easy question to answer in many cases)? What procedures are in place to manage updates and data integrity and security?

- **How is the data managed?** This question covers everything from the formats of data in spreadsheets to database management systems and the issues in the new sphere of Big Data.

Note   This chapter is somewhat different from the others in this book in that it doesn't show you the code to write because most of the issues are at a higher level than the code. In fact, it can be argued that the issues of data management are at least as important as the code that creates, manages, and uses the data. But whatever your opinion on the relative importance of code and data, they are both so important that both belong in any approach to computer science in the twenty-first century. Perhaps fifty years ago when "data" meant carton upon carton of punched cards, reel upon reel of magnetic tape, and stacks and stack of paper documents to be keypunched, it was possible to look at computer science without bothering about all that data. It's not true anymore. As the pioneers of computer programming in the 1940s understood, computers can work with codes that stand for numbers just as easily as codes that stand for program logic and commands. Data and code are, in many ways, interchangeable. That's the lesson of Grace Hoppe: it's what makes compilers possible.

What Is the Data?

If you think the answer to this question is simple, think again. When you read, hear, or see a news item about a data breach, hacking, or system failure, you often find references to data that you never thought about before. When you first start to think about the data that an app uses (creates, generates, or manages), you think clearly of various aspects of that data.

What the news reports often tell us is what many data managers have known for quite a while: that application data is just the tip of the iceberg.

The time and place where someone used the app are important in many cases, and those items are part of the app's data. (If you don't believe this, follow the news items and look for what investigators are searching for when they search for data on a suspect's phone, desktop, or other device.)

Data sent to or from an app can fall into the "app data" category. Also in the category of app data is the app description on an app store along with comments on media (including social media) about what the app can be used for, and how it is used.

All of this is "app data," and all of it matters in various ways to various people. The data that routine users of an app deal with in their routine uses of the app is just part of the app's data.

Everyone needs to be aware of this data whether you are a user, developer, or manager whose job includes using an app and its data. Each role has to think about the app data. Start with the designer or developer. If you start to think about this data, you may decide that you cannot control who keeps track of when and where people use your app.

That's wrong.

The record of use is, in part, generated by the app itself, and that is your responsibility if you are a developer or designer. If your app welcomes returning users with a "Welcome Back!" message, that may be a friendly welcome, but in order to generate it, you as the developer have to store the information that distinguishes between a first-time user and a returning user. Right away, you are storing information that may or may not be important to your users (and to others). Every design decision of this kind affects the app data.

In some cases, it clearly doesn't matter, and in others it does matter and the user knows it. If your app charges per use, it's reasonable that you're keeping track of the uses. In general, many experts in security and data management suggest that you store everything you need and nothing you don't need. "It might come in handy some day" is really not a very good rationale for deciding to store data. Remember that data that is not stored can't be stolen, it can't be garbled or corrupted, and — perhaps most important of all — it can't take up valuable storage space on devices and the cloud.

It is a source of amazement to many developers how clients come in and sit down to discuss a new project with a long list of data to be stored in this new project or app. If the developer asked the client where the data will be stored, the response all too often is "in the app" or, sometimes, "in the cloud." Before you move very far into a project, make certain that you understand exactly where the data will be stored. As you hone in on the details of storing data, clients often start to understand what is entailed. You can give them some estimates for the storage and maintenance of their data, and, many times, the need to store lots and lots of possibly useful "someday" data is reduced or disappears.

Remember: store what you need to store and nothing else. Read histories of famous computer science projects and follow the adventures of projects that have come to grief with overly ambitious data storage schemes. There are many.

The need to clarify data and its storage doesn't mean you shouldn't store data. You must store and use it in most cases. Just be careful.

Where Is the Data Stored?

If you take the broad approach to app data, right away you are considering that it is stored in several places because the usage data will wind up being stored possibly by an Internet service provider and all of the intermediate participants in running the app. Even on a dedicated personal device with no network connection, chances are that the usage data in some form or other is stored in the device. However, moving beyond those cases, you can look at where the app's own data is stored — that is where the data other than the environmental and usage data is stored.

This data is separate from the data used as the app is running (that is, the stack and heap locations that are discussed in Chapter 7).

This is the data that an app may store to keep track of game scores or moves, to manage data ranging from word processing text or spreadsheet data or even recordings that the app makes of music or video). That is the data that needs to be stored somewhere so that users can come back to it when they want to continue working with it (or even when they want to erase it).

The term *persistent storage* is often used for such data storage. The term has its roots in descriptions of storage devices that retain their data even when they are powered off. If you turn off a disk drive, you can turn it on again and use the data. That is persistent storage. If you have data stored in the memory of a device as in the stack and heap, when the app stops running or you power off the device, the data is gone – it's *nonpersistent*.

Note   These are the concepts. Because people so often expect persistence of their data even if the actual storage device or medium is not available, there are ways that hardware and software developers can keep the data available even when the physical storage is not available, so you may observe persistence in what appears to be nonpersistent storage.

There are three main places where this specific app data can be stored (that is, where the data that most users and developers think of when they think of app data). Those places are:

- Storage for the app on the device while it is running.

- Storage for the app on the device that is persistent.

- Storage on the device that is generalized for all apps on the device.

- Storage on storage-focused locations that are designed specifically for storage (Google Drive, Apple iCloud, Microsoft OneDrive and Azure, Dropbox, and the like).

Storing Data in Nonpersistent App Storage

Apps have storage locations that are available to them while they're running. This space is nonpersistent, and the data is not retained after the app stops running or the device is powered down. In fact, computer storage is cheaper than it was, but it is still an expensive and scarce resource. It is reused where possible by the operating systems. In order to reuse data storage when possible, the operating system keeps track of data that is no longer needed. When you "delete" data, you typically cause the operating system to mark the data as deletable: it typically does actually erase the data.

Note   There are options available to actually delete data rather than just mark it as reusable storage space. In fact, secure deletion usually involves writing a random or known pattern over the storage locations to be reused – sometimes repeatedly. It actually is very hard to get rid of data once it has been written somewhere.

Although the reality may be different in some cases, developers generally treat app storage as nonpersistent. To store data after the app ends or to send it to other devices or apps, other techniques need to be taken.

Storing Data in Persistent App Storage

The model of storage on iOS (which includes Swift) has dedicated persistent app storage. This storage is allocated for the app's use, and the app and its developer can do what they want with the storage (although there are size limits to this storage). This is the storage that is erased when you delete an app from your device as you see in Figure 9-1.

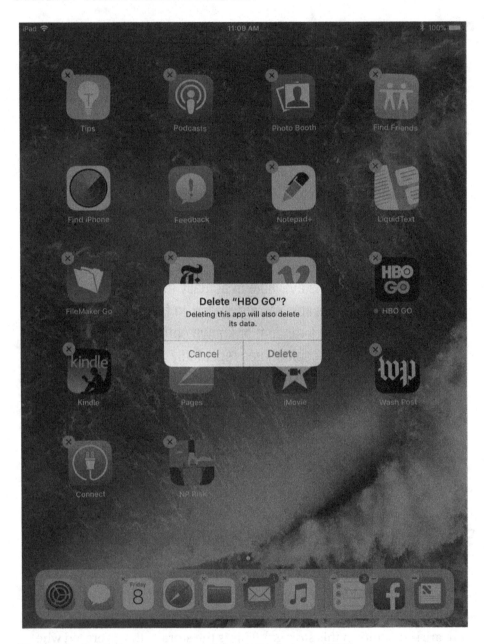

Figure 9-1. Deleting an app deletes its data on iOS

Storing Persistent Data Outside of App Storage on a Device

Apps on all computers from mainframe supercomputers to the tiniest smartphones have the ability to read and write data to persistent storage. This general ability is mitigated by the fact that those features may not be available to every app. In general, storing data on a device in this way is the right way to store data that is specific to a device, app, and user. For example, you can use available storage to store scores in games, data that is entered for analysis, or any other purpose.

These storage locations for apps are often referred to as *sandboxes*. Among the mitigations that limit the possibilities for app reading and writing data, the most common is restricting reading and writing to an app's sandbox.

Note   "Sandbox" is used in several senses. It can refer to a testing area for apps and projects such as the sandboxes that let you test out integration with eBay, Amazon, and the like. In such sandboxes, you can actually test things such as purchases that will not actually be charged to an actual credit card. Sandboxes often refer to runtime nonpersistent data storage for apps such as heaps and stacks as described in the previous section. A sandbox can also be the persistent storage available only to a given app on a given device (or on shared devices with a common user identifier such as an AppleID).

Storing Data in Shared Storage Locations

There are many data storage locations for you to choose from once your look beyond the device on which your app is running. Dropbox, and other cloud services are common resources. Since iOS 11, the Files app on iOS exposes the various locations for files to you as you see in Figure 9-2. If you have Dropbox or other accounts, they show up in Locations. The integrated user interface lets users see the files and their locations no matter where they are. (Remember, that these are all persistent storage locations.)

Figure 9-2. *Use Files to manage files and locations on iOS devices*

Who Is in Charge of the Data?

If you have identified your app's data and where it is to be stored, you still have two issues to resolve: who is in charge of it and how is the data managed and formatted. The issue of who is in charge (discussed in this section) is remarkably untechnical.

If you write an app that lets people store some of their data — perhaps sightings of wildlife along with the date, time, photo, and comments — who is in charge of that data? Who owns it? Who can use it? There many questions.

Although computer science traditionally has focused on design and implementation of computers and computer software, increasingly people who work in the computer science fields are being asked to handle data questions like these. The answers to these questions can be complex (and, in many cases, there isn't agreement as to what the answers may be).

In day-to-day practice of computer science by developers, designers, users, managers, and everyone else who is involved, the issues of data discussed in this chapter may be unresolved. Part of the lack of resolution may be an absence of best practices and even a lack of people who are aware of the issues.

Until such time as there are clear guidelines and standards, the approach to data issues discussed in this chapter seems to be very much haphazard. Many people who work in the field take the position that unless there is some other guidance and standards for a specific project, it behooves someone on each project to raise the issues discussed here and to try to see that they are addressed in each project.

Ownership of Data

There are several aspects to the ownership of data. The most basic is who has ownership in the sense of the legal right to publish (or not publish) the data as well as the right to allow (or disallow) access in means other than publication.

In today's world, there may not be simple answers, but increasingly we find that specific aspects of data ownership are addressed. In documents and agreements of various legal status, people rely on representations about ownership every time they post or view data from a social media site.

The question of ownership often arises when data is put to a new use. If you are using an app to track your wildlife sightings, you may think that your data is your data and that's the end of it. However, if your data is aggregated along with wildlife sightings from other people — perhaps millions of people — that data then may have significant value. That value may be of value to scientists as well as to marketers. In its aggregated form, your spotting of a black squirrel may be useful and valuable.

In building and managing apps, the awareness of ownership often has to be built into the app. The issue of who is the owner of the data may not need to be resolved, but more and more apps are being designed so that if the value of the data becomes significant, the app can support what is needed to profit from that value.

The ways of achieving these results aren't particularly complicated. They may be as simple as making certain that access to data in an app is protected by some mechanism such as passwords or other credentials so that access can be controlled and granted (or not) depending on identity, payment, or some other criterion.

All too often, an app's data design is such that instead of turning on an option to manage access control, major architecture changes to data storage and access are required to manage access control.

Data Integrity

Regardless of who owns data, there needs to be a mechanism in place to secure the integrity of data. Stored data is inherently unstable if only because the movement of data from computer to storage device and back again is one of the weak spots of system development and integration.

In the simplest cases, the connection between computer operations and data storage can be disrupted because the connection is missing (or unstable). Either device can be missing or powered down.

Furthermore, the process of moving data is often fragile. The data ultimately is a sequence of bits, and the integrity depends on each bit's value being accurately preserved during storage and transfer as well as the sequence being similarly preserved.

There are three critical tools for use in managing data integrity:

- Checksums are used to help preserve the representation of the data.

- Timestamps and other data markers are used to record changes to the data

- Version control is used to help identify different versions of data.

Using Checksums

To this end, there are many strategies available to developers and designers. One of the most common and simplest is to use a mechanism such as a *checksum*. In this approach, the binary digits (or, more commonly, the bytes or characters) of data are treated as binary numbers. They are manipulated — often by adding them up — and the result is stored. When the data needs to be verified, the bytes or characters are re-added and that sum is compared to the stored sum (the checksum). This approach, which is often enhanced with further manipulations such as division by prime numbers will catch common errors such as an incorrect bit in a long string of data. In fact, many communication protocols, devices, and standards allow for such checking and automatic retransmission of possibly corrupted data.

A basic understanding of checksums (perhaps in no more detail than this paragraph) is a part of a computer science practitioner's toolkit.

Using Timestamps and Other Data Markers

Beyond the physical integrity of bits and bytes, there is a need to somehow or other preserve the integrity of the data and its changes. Many database designers automatically store a timestamp (the date and time) of the storage of data and its updates.

Timestamps are often expressed and stored as a time interval since a known date. There are several such *reference date*s in common use. (*Epoch* date is a similar term.)

Among the common ones are:

- Midnight on January 1, 1970. This is the reference date used in Unix (and related systems such as Linux and macOS/iOS).

- Midnight on January 1, 2001. This was chosen to reflect 2001 being the year of the first release of Mac OS X (now macOS).

Dates before the reference date are expressed as negative values of seconds. The times expressed are generally in Coordinated Universal Time(UTC), which formerly was known as Greenwich Mean Time (GMT). Thus, these times are constant across the globe.

Along with timestamps, there often are other data markers that are used to identify data and its changes. In addition to timestamps, there are one or more universally unique identifiers (UUIDs). These are often provided by operating systems. They are guaranteed to be as unique as possible across the world. They are typically fairly long strings that you can create through the operating system; you can also add your own identifiers to them so that you have a universally unique identifier of a specific data element. These can be helpful in debugging.

You will find comments that these markers take up valuable storage space and that the computations involved in creating and decoding them use up valuable computing resources.

These are absolutely valid concerns, but remember that their significance has decreased over time with the advent of much more powerful devices becoming the norm.

A common set of data markers is often stored as part of most data items. The elements differ from project to project, but the values usually come from this list:

- Timestamp of data creation (first storage)

- Timestamp of last modification

- Identification of data creation

    1. User

    2. Device

    3. Location

- Identification of data modification

    1. User

    2. Device

    3. Location

- Universally Unique Identifier of the data element.

- Data version

Version Control

No matter how skilled you are and how much experience you have, it is unusual for your design of data storage to not need modifications over time. There may be errors, but even if there aren't, things change. You may need to store different data, and some data that you have stored may be irrelevant.

In order to handle situations like these, it is common to provide an identifier for a data format — that means some identifier of what data is being stored and how it is stored. A common practice is to store the version identifier in the simplest form possible at the beginning of a data record. A simple binary number is sufficient for version management.

If you do this, when your app reads (or writes) data, the first thing read or written is this number. As soon as it is read, the app can then know what else is stored in that record, and it can be read.

With Swift, the way this is often done is to store the version number and follow it with a dictionary (see Chapter 6, "Working with Data: Collections." A dictionary is very flexible so that you can determine what the keys are at runtime or even use the version number to let you know what they are. If the meaning of keys changes with versions (a sometimes unavoidable situation), you have all the data you need to decode or encode the data.

How Is the Data Managed

There are two aspects to data management to consider:

- For external data, where and how it is managed.

- Formatting and structure of data.

Managing External Data

If data is stored externally, that might be on a connected computer or disk drive to which your app has access. More commonly, apps store data in external data providers that specialize in providing storage for apps.

These are special use versions of products such as Dropbox, Google Drive, Box, OneDrive, and iCloud. These are geared to users who want basic file-based storage for the most part.

In addition, there are on-demand hosting services such as Amazon Web Services (AWS), Microsoft/Azure, Google Cloud Platform, Aliyun, and IBM Bluemix/SoftLayer. The difference between these services is that they are geared to use by apps that want to directly access data storage rather than working with files. (Note that this is a basic overview.)

Most modern development environments support Internet-centered protocols like REST that make it easy to read and write data remotely.

Even more important, these on-demand hosting services support various types of software as a services (SaaS) and storage as a service. If your app suddenly takes off and you need to increase your data storage dramatically very quickly, this is what they do automatically.

Their data farms and data centers are located around the world and processing can be passed off from one to the other around the globe and around the clock. This is the way in which rapidly scalable apps are able to be deployed. From the standpoint of the app, the storage is at a single location even though in reality it can be widely distributed for redundancy in case of failures and automated backups.

This bring us back to the basic question of where your app data is. In these modern architectures, you — and no one — may know where it is.

Formatting and Structuring Data

Working with on-demand cloud storage means that you can determine the type of storage that you use: the service only provides the storage.

Common storage protocols and formats come in several groups.

- **Simple and portable.** The most basic formats come originally from spreadsheets. They are text-based formats designed for rows and columns of data. The two most common are comma-separated values (CSV), text (tab-delimited). The data is character-based.

- **JSON**. Java Script Object Notation is a character-based format that structures data into a hierarchical structure (such as students within a class, which is within a school). JSON is a text-based format, so it can be read and written with any tools that work with text. See Listing 9-1 and Figure 9-3 for examples of using JSON with Swift 4.

- **Property Lists**. Apple has a property list (*plist*) design pattern that consists of items with types of String, Number, and Boolean as well as the collection types Array and Dictionary. These can be combined, so a property list might consist of a dictionary that itself contains several arrays and another dictionary. As long as all components are compatible plist types (String, Number, Boolean, Array, and Dictionary), all will be well. There are utility functions that quickly convert property lists to and from formats that can easily be stored. In addition, you can add your own types.

- **Proprietary formats**. These are the formats that traditionally have been used for special purposes in proprietary apps. It is getting to the point where people are leery of trapping their data in proprietary formats. More and more, wise consumers and managers look for the use of common formats or, if proprietary formats are used, the ability to easily import and export data from standard formats.

- **Dashboards and big data**. Along with concern about trapping data in proprietary formats, people are recognizing that they need to combine data that is stored in a variety of systems and formats. To that end, *dashboards* and dashboard tools are being developed. They take the data in whatever format it is and visualize and synthesize it so that a unified picture can emerge. (Tableau is a popular dashboard tool.)

- **SQL and other databases**. Traditional databases tend to use proprietary formats for data storage, but they are unified by their use of SQL as a management and query language. The database management system (DBMS) takes the responsiblity of storing the data, but almost all DBMSs today provide SQL access. In this way, Dashboards and SQL serve similar purposes: providing common access to data stored in various formats.

Using JSON with Swift 4

JSON is rapidly becoming one of the most common formats for data sharing. There have been several iterations of code in Objective-C and Swift that convert to and from JSON (particularly between JSON and the plist types). With Swift 4, those built-in tools have been rewritten and simplified. They are shown in Listing 9-1.

Listing 9-1 shows a Swift playground that takes one of the plist types (an array in this case) and converts it to JSON and back again. This is a common way of sharing data with spreadsheet, databases, and even web browsers (many of them can read and format JSON files).

In Listing 9-1, you see the setup of the playground. Note that Foundation must be imported, but the JSON tools don't require UIKit. They are lower-level tools. A local array is created and then printed out.

```
import Foundation
let myArray = ["one", "two", "three"]
print (myArray)
```

There is a class in Swift 4's standard library that handles JSON conversion. You need to create your own instance of that class:

```
let jsonEncoder = JSONEncoder()
```

The heart of the playground is two lines of code that use the jsonEncoder instance. The first line that is optional specifies in this case that the format of the JSON text should be easy for people to read:

```
jsonEncoder.outputFormatting = .prettyPrinted
```

Next, you use the encodeToJSON instance to encode myArray (or any other plist-compatible type). The result of encoding is stored in this example in encodeToJSON.

```
let encodeToJSON = try? jsonEncoder.encode(myArray)
```

The option spaces the JSON text to make it more readable. In the full listing in Listing 9-1, you'll see the error checking that surrounds this line of code.

In Listing 9-1, encodeToJSON is then decoded using the same jsonEncoder instance:

```
let decodeFromJSON = String(data: encodeToJSON, encoding: .utf8)
```

The UTF8 encoding is a standard text encoding that is commonly used. You can find other encoding values in the documentation.

When you consider that you can encode and decode large arrays and dictionaries into text to read and write, you have a very powerful way of managing data that can be stored for other apps on other devices to read and write.

Listing 9-1. Converting to and from JSON

```
import Foundation

let myArray = ["one", "two", "three"]


print (myArray)

let jsonEncoder = JSONEncoder()

jsonEncoder.outputFormatting = .prettyPrinted

if let encodeToJSON = try? jsonEncoder.encode(myArray) {
  if let decodeFromJSON = String(data: encodeToJSON, encoding:
  .utf8) {
    print (decodeFromJSON)
  } else {
    print ("failed")
  }
  print ("did encode")
} else {
  print ("failed2")
}
```

Figure 9-3 shows the playground code with error checking code added.

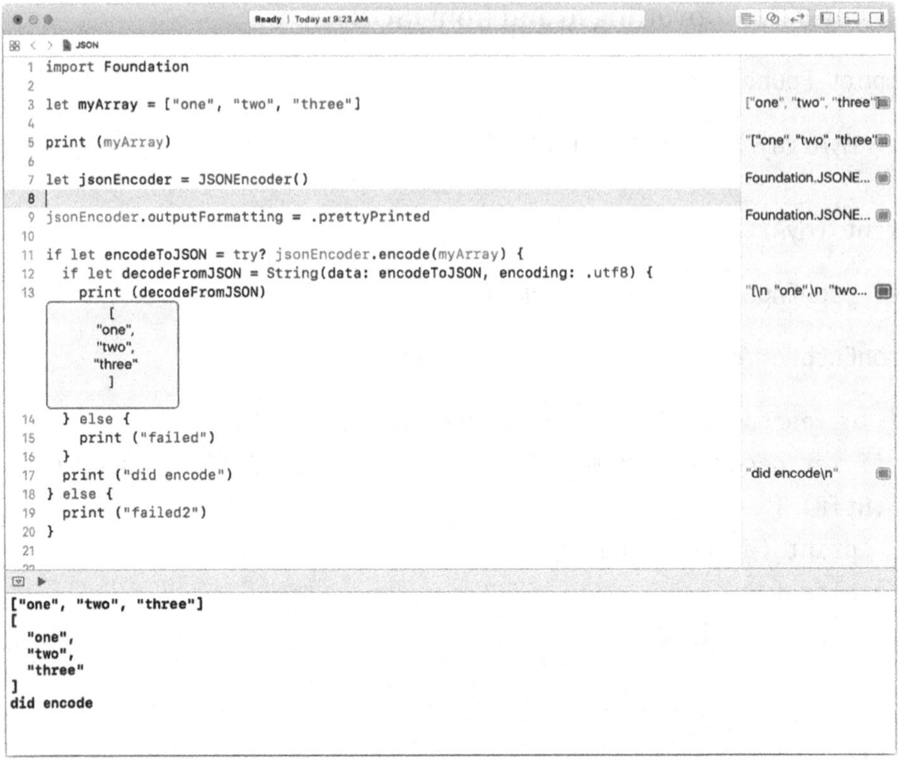

Figure 9-3. *Encoding and Decoding JSON in a playground*

Listing 9-2. Encoding/Decoding JSON (Swift 4)

```
import Foundation

let myArray = ["one", "two", "three"]

print (myArray)

let jsonEncoder = JSONEncoder()

jsonEncoder.outputFormatting = .prettyPrinted
```

```
if let encodeToJSON = try? jsonEncoder.encode(myArray) {
  if let decodeFromJSON = String(data: encodeToJSON,
  encoding: .utf8) {
    print (decodeFromJSON)
  } else {
    print ("failed")
  }
  print ("did encode")
} else {
  print ("failed2")
}
```

Handling Data That Is Not There: Swift Optionals

One of the peskiest issues in computer science is the problem of how to handle data that is not there. This is the case when there is missing data or data that does not exist for any reason. If you leave the data blank, it may be interpreted as a zero if the field is normally numeric. Counting a blank field as zero will throw off averages if they are calculated. Of course, you can simply ignore blank fields and keep your averages clean, but you then have no way of indicating that there is no data for a valid reason. Perhaps the reading on a sensor or gauge is missing because the telemetry or power source has failed. If zero is a valid reading, then there is no way to distinguish between zero-as-missing and zero-as value.

You can always pick another special number to use to indicate missing data. Whatever number you choose can throw off calculations. (Many mainframe computer programs used 99 to indicate missing data, including the data for a year.) A year with a value 99 was unimagined in the 1960s when such programs were often written. In the 1960s when financial institutions were issuing 30-year mortgates and bonds that would mature on or after 1999, this problem grew into the Year 2000 problem.

The only way to indicate missing data is to have some kind of value that indicates whether the data is "real" or not. Different languages and systems handle this issue in different ways. Swift uses *optionals.*

Optionals are written with a question mark; it indicates that the data is of the specified type, but it may not exist at all. Thus a declaration for an optional Int would be written as follows

```
var i: Int?
```

The variable can have any valid integer value; however, it can also have no value. That is represented by nil as in

```
i = nil
```

You can test to see if a variable is nil or not using code such as this:

```
if i != nil ...
```

In Figure 9-4 you see an optional Int variable declared. It is not set to anything, so its value is nil (you can see this in the sidebar at the right of Figure 9-4.

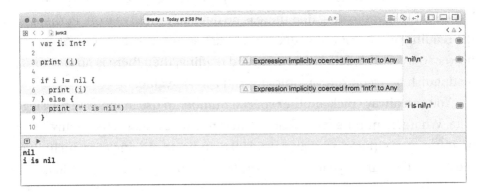

Figure 9-4. *Test for an optional value*

· You can test to see if it is not nil (line 5) and, if so, print it out. Otherwise, you print a message that it is nil.

If you try to use the optional for any purpose, you will get an error as you see in Line 11 of Figure 9-5. Most of the time, this is generated by the playground or Xcode: it won't even compile as you see in Figure 9-5.

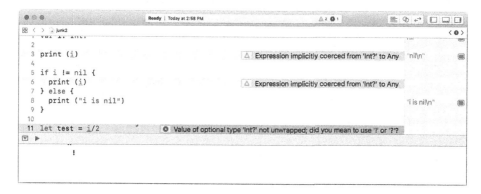

Figure 9-5. *Trying to use a nil*

If you test to see that the value is not nil, then you can go ahead and use it as you see in Figure 9-6.

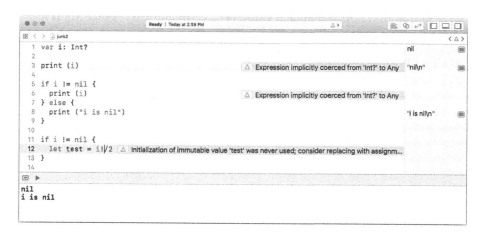

Figure 9-6. *Using an optional*

Even if a variable is declared as optional, you can see set its value. Thereafter, if it is tested to see if it is nil, it will not be nil because it has a value as you see in Figure 9-7. In Figure 9-7, you can see that the debug pane shows the unwrapped value as an optional.

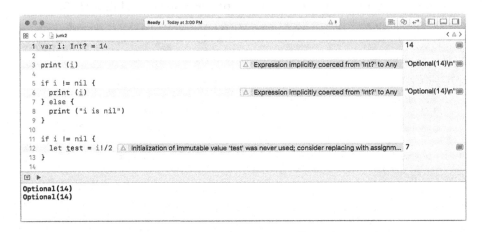

Figure 9-7. *Using optional binding*

Instead of testing to see if an optional is `nil`, you can use Swift's *optional binding*. This lets you write code that may fail because part of it is an optional. If it fails because a value is `nil`, the failure is graceful. If it is not nil, the code proceeds. For example, in Figure 9-8 the code in line 3 starts the optional *binding*:

```
if let unwrappedI = i {
```

This code takes the value i that is declared as an integer, and attempts to set that value to the new variable unwrappedI. If i is nil, setting unwrappedI to the value of nil will fail. The entire clause will be false. Thus, if i is nil in this snippet, this code will evaluate to false:

```
if let unwrappedI = i
```

Execution will continue with the else clause that prints "i is nil."

The process of looking inside an optional to see if it has a value is called *unwrapping*. You perform unwrapping in two ways:

! is forced unwrapping. The optional is treated as its underlying value. If it happens to be nil, you will probably get an error.

? is conditional unwrapping; you use it in optional *binding*.

Figure 9-8 shows how this code behaves when the optional i is set to a value in line 1.

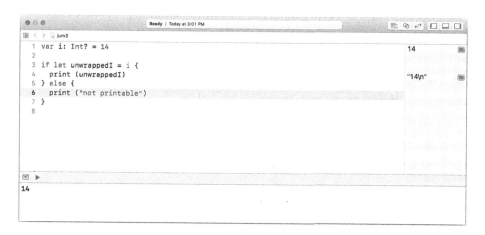

Figure 9-8. *Unwrapping a value*

In Figure 9-9, you see how the code runs when the optional does not have a value.

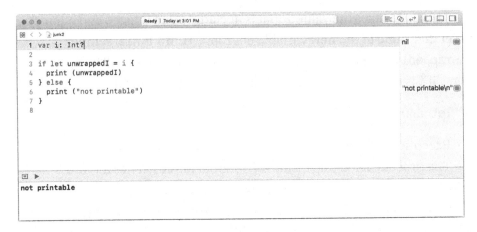

Figure 9-9. *Leaving an optional wrapped*

Summary

Managing app data is a critical part of computer science projects even though it is sometimes taken for granted. In this chapter, you see the basic issues you must be aware of and plan for in your computer science projects. Most of the issues in this chapter aren't code based: they are the basic issues of data management and ownership.

If you want to get back to the nuts and bolts of coding, have no fear. The next chapter, (Chapter 10, "Building Components") has plenty of code to help you understand and build usable projects and components.

CHAPTER 10

Building Components

The basics of working with data and the flow of control can help you write code, but how do you get from there to building something useful? (In fact, this is one of the challenges of traditional programming instruction: people learn on the first day how to write a program that prints out "Hello There," and there's not a clear path from "Hello There" to building Facebook.)

This chapter provides you with a few of the stepping stones from a single line of code to — if not Facebook, at least the tools you'll need to start working in a software environment like that. (Mind you, there are many stepping stones on that journey, and this chapter just provides you with an overview.)

Why Build Components

There's one phrase that sums up a major reason for building components: "divide and conquer." In fact, if you look on the Internet for references to "divide and conquer," you will find that it is the common name for a specific architecture and development process in computer science. The principle is analogous to the divide and conquer (or divide and rule) phrase that dates back several millennia. If you take a large problem (or a large group of people) you can often solve a problem or encourage people to act in certain ways if you break the problem or the group down into small groups or even individuals.

© Jesse Feiler 2018
J. Feiler, *Learn Computer Science with Swift*, https://doi.org/10.1007/978-1-4842-3066-4_10

When it comes to app development, if your goal is to write the next social media app (there's a long line of people waiting to do that, in case you're planning to do that), starting with a blank piece of paper or empty screen isn't going to get you very far. You could break down the app's design into large components — perhaps a handful of less than a dozen. From there, you might subdivide each component; more likely, you would get individuals or groups to work on specific components. Before you know it, you'll have at last the broad outline of how to build a large and complex app.

There are theories and rules aplenty in the world of app design, implementation, and management. A popular methodology (Agile) encourages the development of working software as early as possible in the process as possible. It won't be complete, but it will run. This eliminates the need for multiple documents and meetings to describe the possible development path from the very beginning – something will be running in some way.

The process continues with many iterations but at all times something will be runnable. (In some environments, iterations are limited to a week in length, which means that the steps along the road may be many and small, but if there's a need for backtracking it may not be terribly disruptive.) And if there is a problem along the way, the next runnable version — even if it's a backtracking version — will only be a week away.

The idea of components as a divide-and-conquer strategy and methodologies such as Agile in which small pieces are built and put together reflects the need to get software developed as quickly and efficiently as possible. In both of these methodologies as well as many others, the process of building a large system involves building small components. The components are either decomposed from the whole concept (divide and conquer) or they are small components that become building blocks of the system.

Components have other advantages over building large-scale systems in a single structure. Chief among these advantages are reusability and manageability. Those features are major features of good computer science design.

Advantages of Components: Reusability

When designers break a large system down into components that can be developed separately, not only does it make the overall project simpler in many cases, but it also can mean that some of the components will be reusable. In providing the architecture for an overall system, designers and developers look for components that can serve the dual purpose of advancing the primary project along with a secondary purpose of being able to stand on their own.

Now that we are well into a world in which people are used to using computers, certain operations are becoming common. These range from interface elements to specific types of operations such as login security, saving documents, and the like.

The actual process of developing the overall structure involves looking for places in the design where reusable components can be developed or employed (after all, if they are reusable, they should be reused).

Making components reusable means that they need to be structured for reuse. At the simplest level, that may mean nothing more than greater attention to documentation than for a one-off code component. The value of reusable components is directly related to how reusable they are so documentation and overall structure are keys.

Advantages of Components: Manageability

When a large system is broken down into components that may be implemented by different development teams, it is critical that their behavior is clear. It's not just a matter of documenting what a component does but also a matter of thinking about what side effects it may have on other parts of the larger system.

By being able to identify the functionality of a component, it is easy to move it around on various system diagrams so that you can experiment with its reuse.

Both reusability and manageability are enhanced by structuring components with clear documentation and with a focus on specific actions that they perform. Minimizing assumptions also plays into the picture: ideally, a component should be able to be picked up and used without much if any reprogramming.

The Basic Components of Development Projects

Bear in mind the previous points as you explore the rest of this chapter. It is devoted to explaining the major types of components that you encounter in computer science projects. It also shows you how you can use them for reusability and manageability of systems — including systems that you decompose from a large group of code modules into a structured collection of components.

Subroutines, Functions, Procedures, and Methods

The most common components you find in projects are subroutines, functions, procedures, and methods. Their names differ from one programming language to another, and there are some differences in their structures, but all of them basically are variations on the same theme. They are miniature programs or apps. They receive input, do some manipulations and calculations on the input, and then they generate output.

The general structure is described in this section, with a focus on Swift. This is the overall view, but it does apply to most components. The main parts of a component are the following:

- Name

- Data inputs

- Data outputs

- Implementation — code

- Implementation — documentation

- Side effects and requirements

Naming Components

Each component you create has a name. The names in most languages cannot contain spaces or special characters except for underscore characters. Other rules apply to languages or to usage in a given environment (such as a specific company). Names are chosen for readability and reuse. They often consist of several words that describe what the component will do. When several words are used, they are typically connected with underscore characters or camelcase capitalization (each word is capitalized except the first — `camelCaseFormatting`, for example). If you are using underscores, such a name might be `camel_case_formatting`. You can combine the styles into something such as camelCase_formatting. It is always a good idea to adopt a standard for naming items as well as for using capitalization and underscores (as well as other styles). It's important for people to be able to know what these items are. Remember that in some listing and cross-references, the names may appear in alphabetical order, so you may want to bear that in mind in your naming conventions.

Also, bear in mind that if you are writing code for reuse and are reusing code that others have written, chances are very great that you will be working with code that adheres to various naming conventions. Try for consistency within individual components and, if possible, within related components written in the same organization or group. Don't spend too much time on this: you can't enforce standards on every developer in the world.

Data Inputs

Data for a component can be provided when the component runs. For example, a component that calculates the area of an object might receive two values: length and width. Other components receive streams of data from devices such as real-time sensors like thermometers or from streams of data (such as social media messages like Tweets).

It makes for good programming style and easier maintenance if the inputs to a component can be clearly defined. Length and width are such easy concepts. Sometimes, the amount of data to be provided to a component is large and varied. One way of managing such input data is to format it into a collection like an array, set, or dictionary. Thus, instead of many data observations from a weather station, you might have an array of such observations — that turns the many into one input item. You can also use a more structured collection such as a dictionary where each element consists of a key (the date/time of the observation) and a value (the observation itself).

The clearer the inputs are, the more easily the code can be reused.

Data Outputs

Data outputs are subject to the same concerns as data inputs specifically making the outputs clear in their meaning and in their structure. One specific type of output is worth highlighting. Some outputs are designed specifically to be used as inputs to other components. In such cases, any changes to outputs need to be synchronized with changes to the related inputs.

This is not a trivial matter, because having such a dependency can limit or even preclude the reusability of code on either side (input or output). One common way of avoiding such problems is by assuming that all outputs are going to be used in one way or another as inputs. Thus, the formats and layouts of the outputs may well be designed using known methodologies so that if necessary, outputs from one component can go to a translating component and thence to the desired recipient. The intermediate component then is responsible for the synchronization of input and output data.

Note   This design pattern is shown in the common model-view-controller design pattern used extensively in Swift and Cocoa. The model is basically the data, and the view is the user interface to that data. An intermediate component – the controller – mediates between the model and the view. That structure allows both models and views to be changed as needed: only the controllers need to be modified as a result of changes to model or view.

Implementation – Code

The heart of a component is the code itself. That is what does the work.

Implementation – Documentation

The code itself is not sufficient implementation. The code needs to be documented. Reuse is dependent on good documentation.

Side Effects and Requirements

In building successful components, most developers strive to minimize or even eliminate any dependencies from outside the component. If data is needed, it is good to provide it as input. Relying on the existence of some data or other that is necessary for the component means once again that the component's reuse is limited to situations where that data is available. On the other hand, if necessary data is provided with inputs, it is part and parcel of the component.

Classes

Components like subroutines, functions, procedures, and methods let you write what are in effect small programs with inputs, outputs, and computations and calculations in the middle. Classes are a different type of component. Using the object-oriented technologies developed in the 1960s and later, classes provide a different type of structure for reusable components.

The object-oriented programming paradigm lets you build objects that contain data and functionality in the form of code. The difference is that the paradigm of components harkens back to the earliest days of computers and computer programming where a program would run by reading in its inputs, calculating something, and exporting its outputs. (This is often called *batch processing.*) At the end of the process, the program would terminate. Sometimes, a containing program would be created so that at the end of the process, the next set of inputs would be read and the next set of outputs would be generated (think of a billing system).

Classes and object-oriented programming fit well into a world that is no longer batch oriented. In many cases today, a class contains data or the ability to receive data, it performs calculations, and then exports data. So far that is the same as batch processing, but, in many object-oriented systems the objects stay around. Some data is received, calculations are done, some more data of a different is received, calculations are done, and other operations may ensue. It's not a matter or read/calculate/write in many cases. Rather, an object may be capable of reading, writing, and calculating at various times. Note that this is an observation of a common difference between many batch-oriented components and many classes: it is not a necessary distinction.

Classes are the descriptions of objects; as they are created (*instantiated*) into *instances*, these objects may stay around for a while. The clear distinction between inputs, computations, and outputs in basic components isn't relevant to many objects.

From the perspective of reusability, classes are just as reusable as other components. Classes often contain components themselves. Typically, those components are *functions*; they may also be *methods*. There is a technical distinction between the two, but in practice, the terms are often used interchangeably. (See the sample object-building example later in this chapter.)

With Swift, structs and enumerations are treated much like classes in many ways. There is more on structs and enums in Chapter 8.

Larger Building Blocks

In looking at reusable components including functions, methods, procedures, and classes, modern languages like Swift let you create larger building blocks. Just as classes can contain data and functionality, *frameworks* can contain classes (and their components). The term *framework* is used in several ways in computer science. The most basic way is the same way it is used in English. There is also a specific use in Swift and Xcode that lets you create reusable frameworks that you or others can use in various projects. Cocoa and Cocoa Touch themselves are frameworks. There are frameworks for user interface, audio, document management, and many other commonly used parts of apps. Within the frameworks, you'll find classes, and within the classes, you'll find more classes and functions, and so on.

Looking at Blocks and Recursion

Components of code need to be packaged in one way or another to be used and reused. There are two special cases of code reuse to examine: blocks and recursion.

Terminology: Blocks and Closures

In the Swift documentation, you'll find this definition of a closure:

> *"Closures* are self-contained blocks of functionality that can be passed around and used in your code."

Subroutines, functions, procedures, and methods are all blocks. Compound statements (as described in Chapter 9) also are often blocks. A block is a section of code that can be packaged with or without the formal structure of a procedure, function, method, or class. If it is not part of a formal structure, it may be packaged with brackets (or, in some languages, parentheses).

What is critically important in the Swift definition is that it is "self-contained." When a block of code is used as a closure, if the code in the block refers to variables outside of the block itself, those variables are made available to the block that is now called a *closure* (because it has *closed* around the variables that are needed for the block to execute.

In Swift, all closures are blocks and many blocks are also closures. In practice, many people use the terms interchangeably.

The most common use of blocks is in cases where you want to perform a block of code and you don't know when you want to perform it. Commonly, it is code that you want to perform after some event or another has happened. If that event is out of your control, you don't know when you'll need to execute the block of code.

Using a Closure

Here is a common example of using a closure. It is code that is typically used in `UIDocumentBrowserViewController` to open documents in the Files app in iOS 11 and later.

```
let document = UIDocument (fileURL: documentURL)
// instantiate a subclass of UIDocument
document.open (completionHandler: { (success) in
    if success {
       // show document
    } else {
       print ("no success opening document")
    } // else
  } // end of block
) // end of document.open parameters
```

Here is what the code does.

- Normally, you create an instance of `UIDocument` as the comment indicates. A local variable called `document` (or whatever you want) is typically used in this code.

- You then open the document using the `UIDocument` `open (completionhandler:)` method.

- The argument of the method called `completionHandler` is a block of code that will be called when `open` completes. (This is a common naming convention.)

- The block of code that is the completion handler is enclosed in brackets. The call to open with the completion handler code removed makes this structure clearer:

  ```
  document.open (completionHandler: {...})
  ```

- The content of the block is shown here. When the block is called, a single parameter will be passed in. For convenience, it is named success here; as all parameters, it is enclosed in parentheses.

  Once success is passed in, it can be tested in an if condition that indicates if opening was successful or not. Thus, in this structure, the block is written out and passed into open as the completionHandler parameter. When the open function completes, it has the code available to run in the completionHandler parameter. How long it takes for that code to run depends on the system workload.

```
{
  (success) in
  if success {
    // show document
  } else {
    print ("no success opening document")
  } // else
} // end of block
```

This type of structure makes multi-threading possible. That is, the processing continues in one or more of the chips in the processor until the completion handler comes into play.

In older software, you will often find this type of code implemented using *semaphores*. Instead of waiting for open to finish, the code in older apps might have a small loop that checks periodically to see if open has run.

In the architecture of Cocoa and Cocoa Touch, this structure that relies on *messaging* and *notifications* makes for much simpler code to write in apps and it makes for much simpler and faster code in the operating system itself.

You will find blocks used in many places.

Recursion

Recursion is another aspect of components you should know about. If you have components that can be reused, they can reuse themselves. This lets you write code that is structured and efficient. Be aware that if not used carefully, it can cause problems. When you work with recursive code, unless you find a way to stop the recursion, you can generate a form of *infinite loop* that never ends in theory. In practice, it ends when the app runs out of memory.

Note   Infinite Loop is the name of the street on which Apple's Cupertino headquarters were located for many years. It is not an infinite loop (you can see the entire thing if you stand on the street) but it definitely is a loop. In 2017, Apple completed construction of its new main headquarters near to Infinite Loop. The new headquarters is known as Apple Park.

Building a Function in Swift

In talking about components, the terminology in Swift uses *function* rather than method. In common usage, many people do refer to these items as methods when they are part of a class (this is a legacy from years of usage where the distinction mattered more than it does now). The alternative terms (subroutine and procedure) are not used in Swift today.

A function consists of a name, inputs and outputs, and the code itself. Here's how to create a simple function in a Swift playground. This function will compute an area based on two parameters (length and width).

Start by creating a new playground on an iPad as you see in Figure 10-1. (You can do the same steps on a playground in Xcode, but the interface is different and less interactive.) The empty playground has suggestions for you in the bar at the bottom of the screen. Among the top-level suggestions is func to create a function.

Figure 10-1. *Create a new playground*

Tap func, and the shell of a function is created for you by the playground as you see in Figure 10-2.

Figure 10-2. *Start creating a function*

Name is highlighted in red suggesting you should enter that first. The function body is highlighted in gray suggesting that you attend to that next. Type in the name of the function — area — as you see in Figure 10-3. Tap the body of the function and it is now highlighted in red for you to attend to.

Figure 10-3. *Enter the function name*

The next step would be to enter the function body. There are several ways to do this. Chances are that no matter which route you take, you will temporarily generate an error. (This is common in development.)

The single line of code shown in Figure 10-4 will return the value of length multiplied by width. Neither variable has a value so far, so you'll generate an error (the red dot at the left).

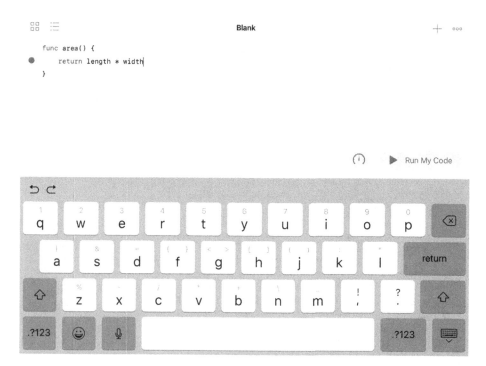

Figure 10-4. *Start building the body of the function*

One way of setting the values of length and width is to pass them into the function as you see in Figure 10-5. (Passing data in with parameters rather than hard-coding it inside the function body makes your code more reusable.)

Figure 10-5. *Pass the parameters into the function*

As you have seen in several code snippets in the book, the way to declare a variable is with a name and a type. Thus, you can declare a length variable (the name) of type Double with

length: Double

Double is the preferred floating point type to use in Swift (rather than Float).

Although the parameters solve the problem of where to get the data, the function needs to indicate in its declaration that a value will be returned. This is the error you see in Figure 10-6.

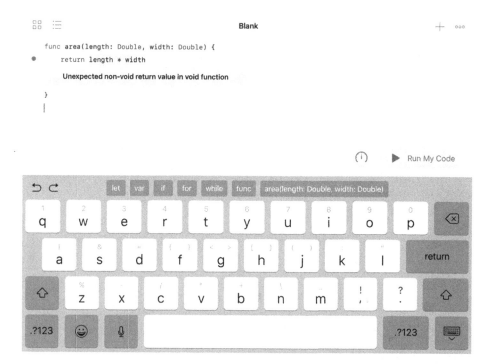

Figure 10-6. *You must declare that a function will return a value*

You can complete the function declaration as you see in Figure 10-7 so that now it intends to return a value.

Figure 10-7. *The complete function*

The return value syntax is

```
-> Double
```

This indicates that it is a return value of type `Double`.

If you want, you can run the code. Nothing will happen, but, in fact, that is fairly good: no errors appear.

Just to recap the steps to build this small function, here they are:

- Tap `func` to create the shell

- Name the function

- Name the parameters passed in and set their types

- Name the return value

- Provide the body that computes the return value

Except for the first step where you create the function shell, you can do these in any order. You'll get errors along the line either because you haven't declared a variable before using it or because you declare it and don't use it. After a while, you'll get used to this sequence.

You can add a line of code to invoke the function. You need to declare a variable and set it to the result of the function. Look on the Shortcut Bar and you'll find `let` (it's just off the screen in Figure 10-8). You often have to scroll along the Shortcut Bar. Tap `let` and you'll get the outline of code you need to use as you see in Figure 10-8.

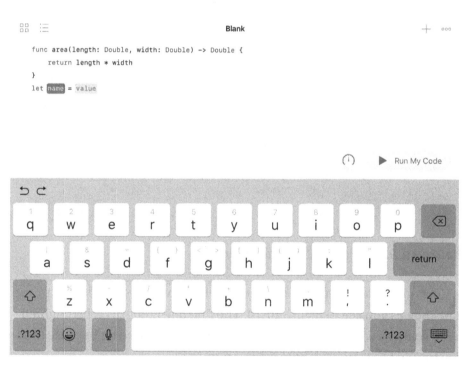

Figure 10-8. *Create a variable to use the function*

Name the variable result (or anything you want), and type in the name of the function as you seen in Figure 10-9. In the Shortcut Bar, the Swift playground shows you the parameters (names and types).

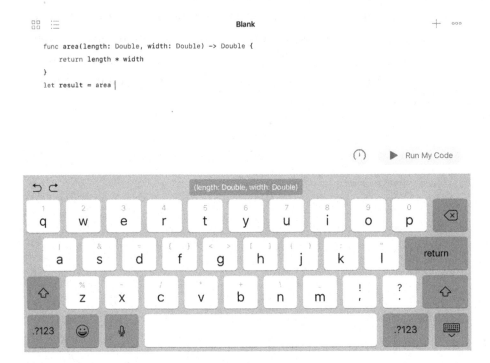

Figure 10-9. *Start to use the function*

Tap on the parameters in the Shortcut Bar, and they are filled in to your code as you see in Figure 10-10. The first one (`length`) is highlighted in red so that's where you start. You get the number popover because the playground knows you want to enter a number.

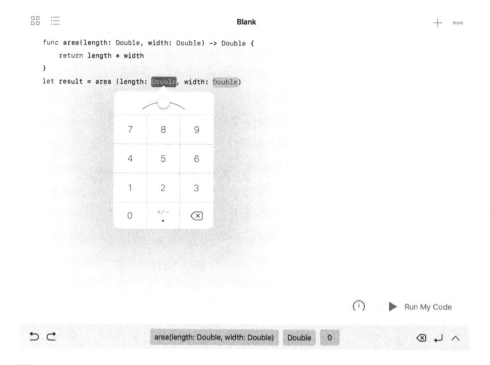

Figure 10-10. *Start entering the parameters*

You'll be guided through each of the parameters with appropriate data entry tools as you see in Figure 10-11.

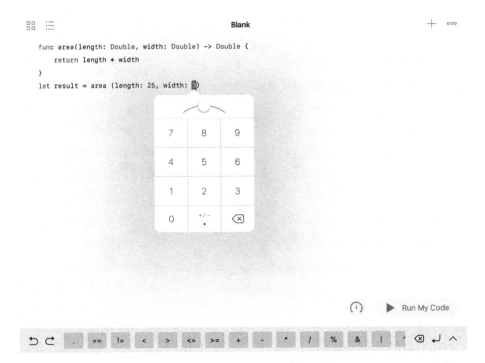

Figure 10-11. *Enter all parameters*

You can now tap Run My Code and see the results as you see in Figure 10-12.

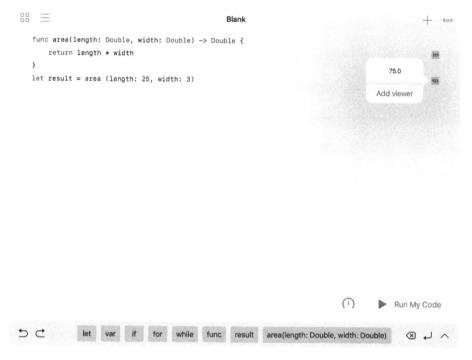

```
func area(length: Double, width: Double) -> Double {
    return length * width
}
let result = area (length: 25, width: 3)
```

Figure 10-12. *Run your code and check the result in a viewer*

Summary

This chapter describes the reasons to use software components and shows you how to construct them in Swift. You see how a Swift playground can walk you through the process of building a function. You can also just type the code into Xcode, but sometimes it's easier to switch between Swift playgrounds and Xcode.

All components have the same basic parts. Here they are presented with the names that you see in a playground.

- name
- inputs (parameters)
- outputs (returned value)
- body (code)

231

CHAPTER 11

Using Events to Guide Actions

Computers have been getting smaller for years. Not only have their components shrunk from vacuum tubes to transistors, there are now entire systems on a single computer chip.

Users control apps. We launch them; interact with the interfaces; and, when we're finished, we shut them down. Sometimes as in the case of iOS, when we don't use them for a while, their data is automatically moved to a safe space to be ready for when we want to use them again. They may never (or rarely) end. They just wait for the next user input.

That's not how things work now, and it hasn't really been true for decades, but mental images take a long time to fade away. More and more, apps are controlled by other apps and even by other computers. When we set an alarm on a computer, another app keeps track of the time and then triggers something on the computer.

You may say that that's just delayed human interaction, but as you start to think of how apps are controlled today, you will find more and more controls that are far removed from human intervention. In general, when you schedule something (perhaps using Siri) using a phrase such as "remind me at...," you're describing something that a computer can set in motion. Whether your "at" is based on time or location, it's easy for a computer to figure out when "at" is true.

233

© Jesse Feiler 2018
J. Feiler, *Learn Computer Science with Swift*, https://doi.org/10.1007/978-1-4842-3066-4_11

When your request to Siri is along the lines of "remind me when…" chances are that there's a more complex process involved in figuring out if "when" is true. (Exclude the special case of "when it is 3:15," which is basically an "at" request.)

What is important about these "when" events is that they come as a surprise to the person who sets them in motion. If you asked to be reminded at 3:15, you may expect that reminder (and maybe even a pre-reminder at 3:00). But "when" events may come with no expectation on the part of the user. You'll see how that works later in this chapter when looking at notifications in Swift and Cocoa.

Where Blocks Fit In

As you saw in Chapter 10, "Building Components," you can modify the normal sequence of command processing by using blocks. The snippet of code here summarizes a common use of blocks. As noted in this chapter, this is common code use in `UIDocumentBrowserViewController` and many other places. The heart of the code is the `document.open(completionHandler:)` function call. It opens the document, and, when the document is opened, the completion handler is called and executed so that you can inform the user that the document has or hasn't been successfully opened and take any other necessary actions (such as updating the user interface with the contents of the document).

```
let document = UIDocument (fileURL: documentURL)
// instantiate UIDocument
document.open (completionHandler: { (success) in
    if success {
      // show document
    } else {
      print ("no success opening document")
```

```
    } // else
  } // end of block
) // end of document.open parameters
```

What is important to remember is that although there is a pause between the call to open and the execution of the closure (either the success branch or the else branch), that sequence is set in the initial code that sets up the block. Unless the code in the block does something unusual, that block will be the code that opens calls after attempting to open the document.

Using Actions and Messaging for Managing Flow Control Summary

It is commonly the case that you want to implement a different type of managing the control flow rather than just waiting to move on to the next step in the predefined sequence. That is where *messaging* comes into play. Messaging lets you dynamically change what is going to be executed — not just when it happens as you can do with completion handlers and closures.

Messaging lets you send some kind of message to a receiver that then acts on it. Looking at the open code that uses a closure, consider the case in which you do not want to specify *what* happens when the document opens or doesn't. A messaging structure lets you send a message to a recipient that will then decide what to do about it. Messaging is used extensively in modern apps for a variety of reasons, one of which is that it helps in building maintainable apps because they don't have to retain all the logical linkages. In the open example, if you want to impost a limit of a maximum of three open documents at a time, you need to know that every open statement must obey that limit both in original coding as well as in maintenance. (It will be very easy to forget to check on that limit when you implement code to open a new type of document.) These issues can be avoided by implementing a generalized opening section of code, but often when you are retrofitting or maintaining code, you don't control how every piece of it is already working. Being able to post a *notification* that something has happened and letting another part of the app *unknown at the time of writing* handle it is simpler. And that's where notifications come into play. Here is a concrete example.

Note   Messaging is widely used today. It is at the heart of *microkernel* architectures for operating systems, and it is key to Cocoa and Cocoa Touch frameworks. Some other frameworks and development tools use different approaches and terminology, but this is what you will find in Cocoa and Swift.

Passing a Button Press/Tap/Click On to... Somewhere

In this example, you'll see how to implement a button that does something that is not known when you write the button management code. This is an overview of the notification architecture. It introduces you to some of the tools in Xcode, the integrated development environment (IDE) used for all Apple tools, but the details of using Xcode are described in the following chapter so treat this section as a preview that focuses on notifications.

Implement a Button with Known Action

To start with, here is the common case of implementing a button that does something that you know about and implement together with the button. This example starts from the Tabbed App starter template build into Xcode. If you create an app based on it, you will have an app with two views as shown in Figure 11-1.

Figure 11-1. *(left) Tabbed App First View and (right) Tabbed App Second View*

The basic template implements two view controllers and the tab bar controller at the bottom that lets you switch between them.

You can add buttons to one of the view controllers along with a label as you see in Figure 11-2.

Figure 11-2. *Add a button and label*

You will see that you can easily write code for the button so that it changes the text in the label as you see in Figure 11-3 where the text has changed to Button Tapped.

Figure 11-3. *Implement the button*

The code to implement the button is not particularly complex particularly with Xcode helping you along the way as you will see in Chapter 12. The code for the button and label is shown in Listing 11-1 and in Figure 11-4.

Listing 11-1. Implementing the button and label

```
import UIKit

class FirstViewController: UIViewController {
  @IBOutlet weak var label: UILabel!
  @IBOutlet weak var button: UIButton!
```

```swift
@IBAction func buttonAction(_ sender: Any) {
  label.text = "Button Tapped"
}

override func viewDidLoad() {
  super.viewDidLoad()
  // Do any additional setup after loading the view,
  typically from a nib.
}

override func didReceiveMemoryWarning() {
  super.didReceiveMemoryWarning()
  // Dispose of any resources that can be recreated.
}
}
```

Figure 11-4. *Code for First View Controller*

The code begins by linking the objects in the interface (using a *storyboard* as described in Chapter 12) to the code. The label and button are both @IBOutlet items — that means that they are in the interface but can be addressed from code. You will see that one is the label and the other is the button.

A similar style applies to @IBAction. That is the code that implements the action for the button. You will see @IBOutlet and @IBAction throughout code that implements the user interface.

The @IBAction line of code can be reformatted so that it is clearer:

```
@IBAction func buttonAction(_ sender: Any) {
  label.text = "Button Tapped"
}
```

When the button is tapped, buttonAction is called and the text of the label changes to Button Tapped.

That is all that it takes to implement a button and its action.

Implement a Button with a Notification

If you want to add a button that will update a label on the second view controller, things get a little more difficult. It's not hard to add a new button to the first view controller that will start the process in motion. Figure 11-5 shows what that will look like.

Figure 11-5. *Add a button to use a notification*

You can also add a label to the second view controller as you see in
Figure 11-6. This will be the label that is updated by the notification button
on the first view controller.

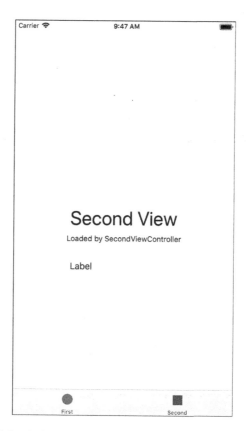

Figure 11-6. *Add a label to the second view controller*

You can start to add the functionality to the button that will update the label in the second view controller, but you immediately run into a problem as shown in Listing 11-2 and Figure 11-7.

Listing 11-2. Code for notification button

```
import UIKit

class SecondViewController: UIViewController {
  @IBOutlet weak var label: UILabel!
  override func viewDidLoad() {
    super.viewDidLoad()
```

```
    // Do any additional setup after loading the view,
    typically from a nib.
}

override func didReceiveMemoryWarning() {
    super.didReceiveMemoryWarning()
    // Dispose of any resources that can be recreated.
  }
}
```

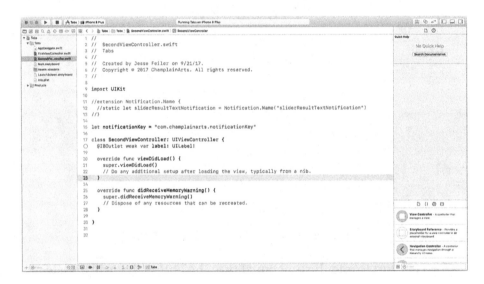

Figure 11-7. *Code for second view controller (Xcode)*

The problem is that the declaration of the navigation button is in the first view controller, but the declaration of the label that needs to be updated is in the second navigation controller. How do you get from the first view controller to the second view controller?

In this case, there are a number of ways to work around the problem. The most obvious is to put the code into an object that connects to both view controllers. That would mean that managing the buttons and labels would move either into the app delegate or into the tab bar controller that manages the two visible view controllers. Either of those strategies will work, but the cost is that the app delegate or the tab bar controller will become more complex. (In the case of the tab bar controller, it is the difference between using a basic UITabBarController as in the template and implementing a subclass so that you can modify one or both buttons or labels from the subclass.)

As a general rule, added complexity is the cost you pay for mixing data and interface elements. The solution is to use a notification.

Notifications consist of two components. The first broadcasts a notification that an event has happened. The second component is an observer that waits to find out about a notification. What is important is that these do not have to know about one another. In the case of the button and label in the first view controller, the communication is within that view controller. With a notification, it can be generated by the first view controller (where the notification button is) and observed by the second view controller (where the label is).

Notifications are broadcast across an app; an object can request to be notified of specific notifications, but there is no direct linkage as there is among objects within a single view controller.

It is this lack of linkage that makes notifications so useful. It also exposes an issue that you will see in the code that follows (along with the solution).

Notification Basics

There are two key points to remember about notifications.

- **Each notification has a name**. This is not a string, but rather a Notification.Name type. You'll see how to specify this.

- **Notifications may not be delivered.** Because there is no direct linkage between notification and observer, if a notification is not observed, no error is generated. The notifier posts a notification, and it may or may not be observed.

Posting a Notification

The first step in the process of implementing the notification button is to post it. Here is the standard code for posting a notification. It will be the action for the notification button in the first view controller.

```
@IBAction func notificationButtonAction(_ sender: Any) {
  NotificationCenter.default.post(
    name: Notification.Name(rawValue:notificationKey),
    object: nil,
    userInfo: nil)
}
```

In this simple case, you need only have a name for the notification. That is done in this line of code:

```
name: Notification.Name(rawValue:notificationKey),
```

That line refers to a variable declared in any area of your app (perhaps in a globals.swift file) with the following code:

```
let notificationKey = "com.champlainarts.notificationKey"
```

Together, those two lines convert a string into a `Notification.Name` type.

That's all you have to do to post a notification from a button action (or any either event).

Observing a Notification

To observe a notification, the object that wants to observe it needs to register and then take some action. To observe a notification, here is the line of code (it's in the second view controller).

```
NotificationCenter.default.addObserver(
  self,
  selector: #selector(SecondViewController.
  didReceiveNotificationResultText),
  name: NSNotification.Name(rawValue: notificationKey),
  object: nil)
}
```

That line of code specifies that if a notification with the given name arrives, a specific function should be called (it is defined as a #selector).

```
@objc func didReceiveNotificationResultText () {
  label.text = "Received Notification"
}
```

Once this setup is completed, the navigation button in the first view controller can cause the label in the second view controller to be renamed. Neither controller knows about the other, and the button doesn't know about the label. This means that if the observer's action in response to the button being clicked is something entirely different (that is, not setting a label's text), it should all still work.

Adding the observer should be done by an object that will be able to act on the notification, so that code will go in that place. Your first guess might be to put it into the viewDidLoad method of the second view controller.

If you do that and run the app, you'll see a problem. viewDidLoad in the second view controller isn't called until the second view controller is displayed. Thus, if you run the app and see the (default) first view controller with its navigation button, tapping that button will send the notification, but since the second view controller hasn't been displayed yet, viewDidLoad has not been called and the observer isn't ready.

You can verify that this is the case by tapping the second view controller tab, which will force viewDidLoad to be called and the observer will be set up. Thereafter, the navigation button will work as you expect.

Summary

This is a common problem, and it will be explored in Chapter 12 as Xcode is explored.

CHAPTER 12

Getting into Xcode

Previous chapters have covered many of the basics of computer science. You've found some Swift playgrounds and snippets of code that illustrate many of the concepts and issues. The focus of this book is on Swift and the basic frameworks of iOS and macOS — Cocoa and Cocoa Touch.

To actually develop in these environments, you will need to use Xcode, Apple's integrated development environment (IDE). This chapter will give you a general overview of how apps and other pieces of software are built in general (that is, not just on these platforms and with Xcode). Then you'll find a focus on how to begin development of an app with Xcode — this will provide more detail of the overview discussed in Chapter 11.

There is a lot to Xcode and the various Apple frameworks, but the focus of the following part of the chapter will be a real-life case study of analyzing a problem in the code for Chapter 11. You have a leg up, because that problem was described in Chapter 11, but in this chapter you'll find a walkthrough of how to find and identify what the problem is and how to fix it. Many developers believe that no amount of book- or class-learning can compare to what you learn when you actually have to diagnose and fix a bug.

© Jesse Feiler 2018
J. Feiler, *Learn Computer Science with Swift*, https://doi.org/10.1007/978-1-4842-3066-4_12

How to Write Software

Many people think that writing software means sitting down with a blank screen or blank piece of paper and typing away. When you've typed enough code, you have an app. This may have been true in the mainframe era with punched cards, but it's not true now.

An app today typically consists of code, graphical elements, other forms of media (video, audio, and the like), as well as an enormous amount of code in several frameworks that become part of the app. The framework code handles routine functionality such as reading and writing data, managing screen and mouse or trackpad, and much of what makes a modern app a modern app.

This means that "writing" an app now starts to mean putting an app together from a wide variety of components and pieces. Although the mechanics of building an app are a separate topic than computer science, a brief overview is worth considering so that you understand how the pieces fit together.

Start by registering for an Apple developer ID at developer.apple.com. You will walk through the process of registration. Note that if you are below the age of majority (adulthood) in your region, you will need an adult to vouch for you. If you are enrolled in a school or work for a company, they may have an Apple developer account you can use.

Here is a generalized sequence of the steps in app development on Xcode. You'll see how to start the process in the following section, "Developing an App with Xcode." These are the questions you will have to answer, so start thinking about them before you begin.

1. **Decide what the app will do.** Sitting down to "write an app" without knowing what that app will do is futile. Whether you are working as an independent developer, part of a corporate team, or in any other configuration, having what is known as an elevator

speech to sum up your project in a few seconds is a good idea (many people would say it's essential). Your purpose or objective may change over time, but that's normal. Just make sure that you know what today's version is. (Note also that periodically during the development process you may want to think about versions.) Modern development technologies like Agile suggest that at all times there should be something runnable, and that is a good practice to follow. This may mean that periodically — maybe even once a week — you have to take stock and either eliminate some functionality or postpone it to a future version in order to have next week's version of the app on schedule.

2. **Begin the app description**. In addition to your 10-second version of the app's purpose, many people (including the author) suggest that you start building the app's App Store presence. That is structured text and images that are more extensive than your elevator speech version. If you will be marketing your app yourself, you will need this sooner or later. If other people do the marketing, you can work out this description with them. The main reason to start this description at the beginning is that it provides more detail for you as you are building the app. Look on developer.apple. com for more information on building your app's online presence.

3. **Name the app.** This can be a code name or a name that you plan on changing later (when you think of a better one). It is easy to change the name that will appear in marketing materials and the App Store. (This is a change from the beginning of the App Store.)

Figure 12-1 shows the General tab for the app in Xcode where you will provide this information.

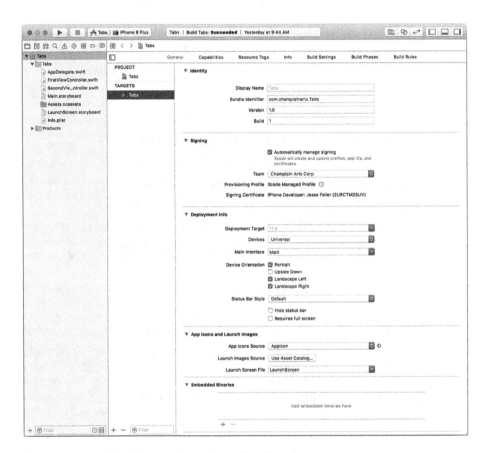

Figure 12-1. *Set General settings for the app*

Display name is the name people will see for your app. (In this example, it is Tabs.)

The bundle identifier is the internal name for the app. It can be different from the Display Name. The bundle identifier must be a unique name. It is normally constructed from your developer account name.

Each version of the app (a *build*) will have its own version and build identifiers. You usually start with version 1.0 (you may prefer something like 0.1) and build 1. Each time you submit an app build to the App Store, you will increase the build counter so that it is always unique and increasing. You can skip build numbers, but you can't go backward. The version numbers will appear to users so it is up to you and your managers and marketers when to decide that the next build will be something like 2.0 rather than 1.16.

Using default values in Xcode are fine until you need to work with the App Store.

4. **Choose the app environments**. Will you run the app on iPhone, iPad, Apple Watch, tvOS Mac, or other devices? What orientation(s) will you support for iPhone and iPad? These are choices you need to make at the beginning (and they are required for the app description). The choices are modifiable, but you need a starting point.

   Choose these in Deployment Info as shown in Figure 12-1.

5. **Choose the earliest app environment version you support**. The default versions in Xcode usually adhere to Apple's policy of supporting the current and one prior version. Thus, with the release of iOS 11 in 2017, iOS 10 is generally supported. Some apps support earlier versions.

   This is also set in Deployment Info using the Deployment Target drop-down list. You can use the default values for the rest of the settings in Figure 12-1.

6. **Choose the app development environment**. Xcode is a given for the Apple frameworks, and Swift is usually a given these days. If you are incorporating third-party frameworks for your development, you may not be able to use Swift but as this is written, the legacy Objective-C frameworks are becoming fewer and fewer. You also need to choose the Xcode development version you want to support.

   This will be set when you set up your project. It is discussed in "Developing an App with Xcode" next in this section.

7. **Decide on the graphics**. You may work with a designer to develop what the app should look like. Also start considering an app logo.

8. **Choose the capabilities you will support on the Capabilities tab as shown in Figure 12-2**. These can be changed later, but this gives you an idea of what you can build in. (Note that it's easier to choose capabilities now and not use them than to retrofit them later in most cases.)

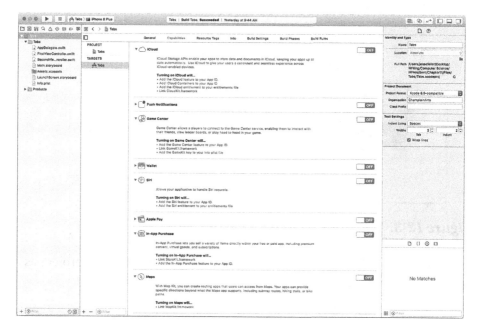

Figure 12-2. *Set capabilities*

Developing an App with Xcode

With your app plans in mind, you can start to actually develop an app with Xcode.

Setting Up the Project

Here are the steps to begin with.

Begin by launching Xcode. You can download it for free from the App Store. Use About Xcode to check the version of Xcode you have installed as you see in Figure 12-3. Note that Xcode build identifiers that tend to be more complex than the simpler style most developers use for numbers like 1, 2, 3, and so forth.

Figure 12-3. *Version 9.0 build 9A235 of Xcode*

Choose New ➤ Project from the Xcode menu to begin your project as you see in Figure 12-4.

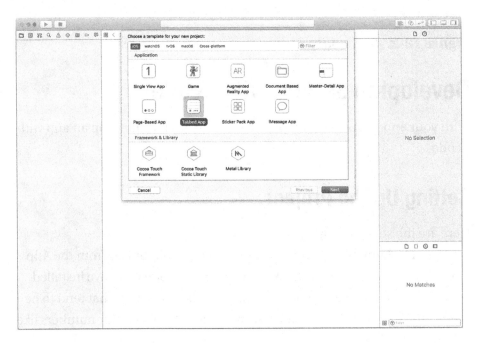

Figure 12-4. *Create a new project*

You will be able to choose a template to start with. In this chapter, Tabbed App is used. When you have time, explore the other templates by creating projects with them. You can always delete them after you have experimented with them.

You will be prompted to select a location on disk for your project. The project will then open in Xcode. You'll see it in a window like that in Figure 12-1. You can use the settings in the top right to show and hide the various parts of the window. (There's more on navigating with Xcode on developer.apple.com and the in-app help.)

Figure 12-5 shows the app at this point. Note that in Figure 12-1, the Utilities at the right are not shown, but they are shown at the right of Figure 12-5. Most developers show and hide the panes of the Xcode window as they work.

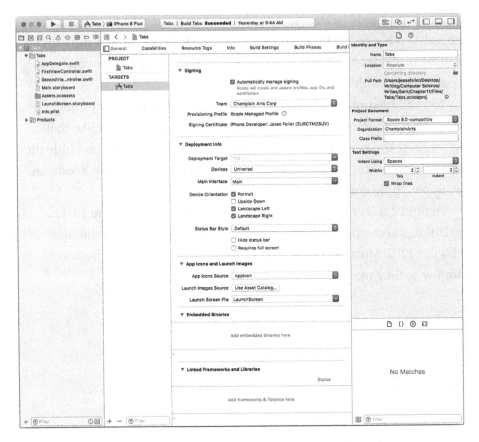

Figure 12-5. *Review the app*

With just a few clicks or taps, you can create a new project in Xcode, but look at Figure 12-6 to see the number of files and folders that you have created. Unless you are well-experienced with Xcode, do not move or rename the project files: leave them where Xcode put them. The two most important components are the xcodeproj file (shown at the bottom of the list in Figure 12-6) and the project folder (Tabs in this case). If you collapse the folders, you'll see that the project consists of the xcodeproj file and the project folder. Those two items can be moved together to another place, but they must be next to one another in a folder (or on the desktop).

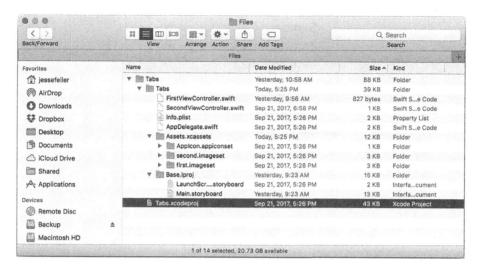

Figure 12-6. *Browse the app's files*

Testing the Project (without Modifications)

If it is not already open, launch the project in Xcode by double-clicking Tabs.xcodeproj. That should open the window you've seen before. Remember that you may have to use the controls at the top right to show or hide the parts of the main window. Figure 12-7 shows you the View menu that you can use instead of the controls at the top right.

Figure 12-7. *Explore the View menu*

Show or hide parts of the main window. If you want to explore them, use this View menu to show or hide them, and you'll be able to match the terminology to the sections of the Xcode window you're looking at.

Use the arrow at the top left of the main window (shown in Figure 12-5) to build and run the app. You should see the results in Figure 12-8 (left and right).

Figure 12-8. *Build and run the app*

Adding the Code and Interface

Once you are satisfied that a template works properly, you can add your modifications. As you saw in Chapter 11, you can add interface elements to your app in the files and folders created as part of your project, not the folder called base.lproj. This folder will be in most of your projects. It contains the interface elements. Today, those are built using *storyboards*. (In the past they were built with `xib` and `nib` files.)

The base.lproj folder consolidates all of your interface elements in one place so that you can easily localize them.

The storyboards give you a graphical tool to draw your interface and connect it to your code. This section provides a very brief overview for you: there is more in the Xcode documentation and at developer.apple.com. There is also a lot of information on the Web, but make certain that it is recent: there is a lot of old code out there.

If you click on a storyboard in Xcode, it will open and you will be able to edit your interface. There already is an interface (that's what you see when you run the template as shown in Figure 12-8). Inside the main storyboard, you'll see a schematic view of the interface as you see in Figure 12-9. (This view includes some elements that have been added — they were added in Chapter 11 and you'll see more about how to add them later in this chapter.)

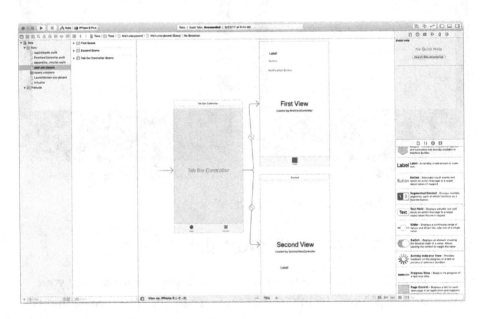

Figure 12-9. *main.storyboard*

At the bottom of the utility area at the right of the window, you see a list of the objects that you can drag onto the storyboard. You don't have to draw anything — just drag.

The elements of the interface are *scenes*, and they are implemented in code by *view controllers*. Most view controllers are visible, and that is the case here. In the Tabs template, there are three view controllers: the first and second views, and a tab bar controller that controls them as you tap the buttons. The tab bar controller appears at the bottom of both view controllers.

As you build your interface with objects from the utility area, you can switch to the Assistant editor as you see in Figure 12-10. (You use the two interlocking circles in the top right of the main window to do this.) Assistant editor leaves the storyboard on the left side and shows the relevant code on the right side of the window. You control drag from an interface element to the code. You will be prompted to name the element in the code. A filled-in circle indicates that the code is connected to the interface. When it is connected, hovering over the interface will show you the name of the connected code element as you see in Figure 12-10.

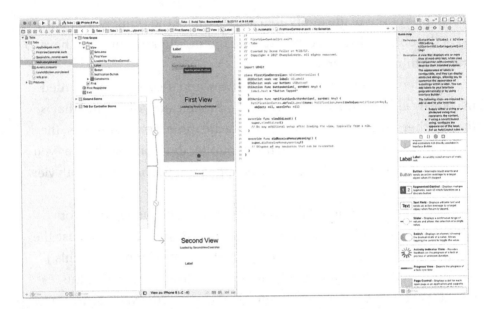

Figure 12-10. *Connecting the interface to code*

This is the key part of linking the code to the interface.

If you want to troubleshoot your connections, one simple way is to control click on the relevant view controller in the storyboard to bring up the view controller connections shown in Figure 12-11.

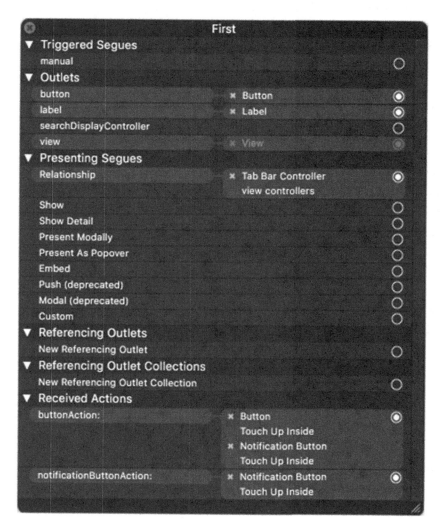

Figure 12-11. *View controller connections*

Explore the interface and the elements to get a feel for this critical part of building an app for iOS or mac OS.

The code that was introduced in Chapter 11 builds on the user interface. It is repeated here for convenience. Listing 12-1 is the code to post a notification.

Listing 12-1. Post a notification

```swift
import UIKit

class FirstViewController: UIViewController {
  @IBOutlet weak var label: UILabel!
  @IBOutlet weak var button: UIButton!
  @IBAction func buttonAction(_ sender: Any) {
    label.text = "Button Tapped"
  }

  // POST THE NOTIFICATION
  @IBAction func notificationButtonAction(_ sender: Any) {
    NotificationCenter.default.post(
      name: Notification.Name(rawValue:notificationKey),
      object: nil,
      userInfo: nil)
  }

  override func viewDidLoad() {
    super.viewDidLoad()
    // Do any additional setup after loading the view,
    typically from a nib.
  }

  override func didReceiveMemoryWarning() {
    super.didReceiveMemoryWarning()
    // Dispose of any resources that can be recreated.
  }
}
```

Listing 12-2 shows the code to observe the notification.

Listing 12-2. Observe a notification

```
import UIKit

let notificationKey = "com.champlainarts.notificationKey"

class SecondViewController: UIViewController {
  @IBOutlet weak var label: UILabel!

  override func viewDidLoad() {
    super.viewDidLoad()
    // Do any additional setup after loading the view,
    typically from a nib.

    // OBSERVE THE NOTIFICATION
    NotificationCenter.default.addObserver(
      self,
      selector: #selector(SecondViewController.
      didReceiveNotificationResultText),
      name: NSNotification.Name(rawValue: notificationKey),
      object: nil)
  }

  override func didReceiveMemoryWarning() {
    super.didReceiveMemoryWarning()
    // Dispose of any resources that can be recreated.
  }

  @objc func didReceiveNotificationResultText () {
    label.text = "Received Notification"
  }
}
```

Testing the Project (with Modifications)

Start to test the app again, and you will periodically encounter a problem. It may be a pesky one for you to solve because it appears to be erratic. The debugging tips in the next section show you how to proceed.

Debugging an App with Xcode

With your buttons and code in place, you'll see that if you click the navigation button in the first view controller, nothing seems to happen. The first step in debugging is to use a *breakpoint*. This causes the app to stop at a designated spot. The simplest way to proceed if you are not seeing something happen that should happen is to set a breakpoint on the line of code that is causing the problem (in this case, by not running). You set a breakpoint by clicking in the *gutter* at the left of a line of code as shown in Figure 12-12.

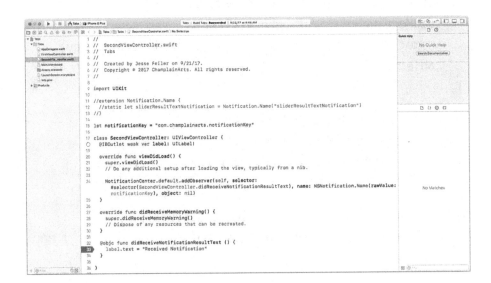

Figure 12-12. *Set a breakpoint*

Run the app again, click the navigation button, and wait for the breakpoint to be triggered.

It won't happen.

All of this and you have confirmed what you already saw, but now you have added the fact that it's not just that the notification isn't acted on, it's never received.

In a case like this, a common practice is to back up. What should have called the `didReceiveNotificationResultText` function?

Because this is a small snippet of code, the answer is right in front of you on line 24: that's where the notification observer is set up. Set a breakpoint there and see what happens when you run the app again.

The result is the same: this line of code is not being called so the observer is not set up.

At this point, you have to do a little thinking to figure out how that can have happened. If you think or do research or ask colleagues about this, you'll probably get the same answer from everyone: if the code is not called, then the function that it is in is not being called (`viewDidLoad`). That may make no sense because you can see the second view controller.

With both breakpoints still set, you can do some more experimenting. What you'll find is that the second view controller's `viewDidLoad` function is called just before it is displayed. If you run the app and click the navigation button in the first view controller, the observer is not yet set up. Use the tab at the bottom of the view to switch to the second view controller to force the view to load, and then go back to the first view controller and try it again. You'll see that now the notification works properly.

This is a very common problem (and a very common class of problem). It is not limited to iOS or Cocoa: this type of problem and debugging technique is common.

The solution is that the observer needs to be set up before a notification is generated. This means that the observer has to be placed in some part of the app that is present right at the beginning. You may consider making `AppDelegate` the place for the observer (and it is commonly used to receive notifications for just this reason).

Summary

This chapter shows you the basics of Xcode so that you can get started implementing the ideas and concepts of computer science in apps. Swift playgrounds are an invaluable way of experimenting, but there are some features that require more complex features that you need to start building your own apps.

As noted, the concepts of debugging described in this chapter are not unique to iOS or Cocoa. You can use then in most languages and environments.

CHAPTER 13

Bringing in People

The field of computer science is often thought of in purely computer hardware and software terms. Somewhere, we as a society need to look at how people are involved because they are the users, creators, managers, and funders of computer science projects.

This chapter looks at the people side of computer science with a focus on the world of apps. Although the issues and principles described here apply to projects that may appear not to involve people (interplanetary space missions, control software for electric grids and generators), there are people involved if only in the management and funding of those projects.

However, the focus in this chapter is more on the projects that you are likely to work on with your knowledge of computer science. First is a quick overview of the formal idea of what is and isn't computable; then you'll find a list of the questions to ask and answer about a specific project you may be developing. These are the questions that have to be resolved

Computability for People

The core of computer science is the idea of *computability*. Simply put, computability is a problem that can be solved with systematic steps. This is different from an algorithm in that algorithms tend to be focused on smaller areas than the computability problems. Thus, the solution of a computability problem may include one or more algorithms.

© Jesse Feiler 2018
J. Feiler, *Learn Computer Science with Swift*, https://doi.org/10.1007/978-1-4842-3066-4_13

Note   If you talk to various people, you'll find out that there are several candidates for "core" of computer science, and computability is one of them. It is particularly useful now because a lot of the current tools for teaching computer science to young people (even preschoolers) focus on computability.

There are two basic types of computable problems:

- **Decision problems**. Given a collection of items, is an item part of that collection or not? Is this invoice part of the set of unpaid bills? Is the user ID authorized to log in? These are problems with a yes-or-no answer.

- **Function** or **computable problems**. These are problems that need to be calculated. What is the product of X times Y?

Other types of computable problems are optimization problems (how best to do something — often how best to compute the answer to one of the two basic types given specific data) and search problems. Problems are often decomposed into sub-problems so that even the most complex problem can be broken into computable pieces.

The main reason for thinking about computable problems is to be able to say with some confidence (and based on some logical analysis) that a particular problem is or isn't computable. That, after all, is the first question people consider when they are thinking of putting their knowledge of computer science to work: Can computer science help me solve this problem?

The Development Questions

You can find many guides to app development on the Web and in various publications. The following six questions are the ones that need to be answered at the beginning of any computer science project. If you can't answer these questions, you will sooner or later come to problems in your project. Someone who is experienced in the use of computer science is expected to be able to help put projects together. That may not be part of a formal curriculum, but it is part of the real world. (If you talk to someone about a potential job where "computer science" is one of the requirements, a familiarity with the development process is usually as important as knowledge of the terminology.)

The six questions may seem too simple to you if you're chomping at the bit and wanting to write code, but they have to be answered before you and others invest time, energy, and money in a project that is not clearly fleshed out. More details of each question (including how to answer it) are found later in this chapter.

Tip   As you start to answer these questions, remember that you can always change your mind, and, in fact, you should plan to change and evolve your answers as any computer science project evolves.

Here are the six questions:

- What are you doing?

- Who is it for? Who will build it, use it, manage it, maintain it, and fund it?

- Why are you building it? Why will people use it?

- When will the project take place? When will it start, and when will it end?

- Where will the project run? What device(s) will it run on; will it require other computer resources such as a web server or database?

- How will you know the results of the project?

What Are You Doing?

The project may be about building an app, but it could be about building an open data resource so that other people can build apps that run on the public data. Many people suggest that this question should be able to be answered in 10 seconds (it's sometimes called an *elevator speech* suggesting that it's what you would say if you found yourself in an elevator with your boss or someone else important and you have the amount of time it takes the elevator to go one floor).

If a friend says, "What are you working on?," most of the time the answer should be only a few seconds long. It is absolutely amazing how hard it is for many people to answer that question. If you can't describe the project simply, chances are you can't implement it. Even the most complicated projects can be summarized: land an unmanned spacecraft on Mars. That's a simple description of a very complicated (and successful) set of missions.

Who Will Be Involved?

Who will do the work on the project, and who will use the end result? Are you building an app for your own benefit so you learn how to build an app and build your portfolio of projects? Is it a project for a job you have or want to have? Will the users be adept users of mobile devices (if that's what you're using) or will they be people who have 400 games on their mobile device but don't know how to change Settings? Will they be people who are adept at using mobile devices but have never used a desk- or laptop personal computer? (Yes, the number of people without experience with personal computers is growing.)

Who will manage or lead the project? In many projects, a team works together. More and more we are seeing collaborative cross-disciplinary projects that benefit from the structured interaction of people from different fields. If you're not familiar with data science and the projects that use it, you might look for references to data science on the Web. There are many examples of successful projects, most of which involve the development or use of computer science technologies.

Why Will People Be Involved?

This boils down to the benefits that people will derive from the project. Are they working on it to get a grade, get a job, make money? The motivations for people who will use the project are typically different from the motivations of people who develop it.

When Will It Happen?

This is actually one of the most difficult questions to answer. In the non-digital world, it is pretty easy to determine when a project is finished: a dignitary cuts the ribbon, a band plays, and the bridge is open. Everyone can see that.

Software isn't visible. In the old days of shrink-wrapped software, people could see the packages in a store, and that certainly made the project seem complete. Determining when the project happens requires you to pull together the answers for What, Who, and Why along with any changes you have made.

There's a new perspective on What Are You Doing? With the additional information you have from the previous questions, now that question can be refined: what are you delivering?

In the world of product development (and especially software development), a common phrase is *minimum viable product* or MVP. There are various interpretations of this phrase, but it generally is taken to mean something that runs and performs the basic functions you expect in the final product.

This may mean that error messages are not complete (which may mean that the app may crash if not used carefully). It may mean that some options are not yet implemented. But it means that you can show someone what "it" is without using a slide presentation: there is something that will run.

One interpretation of minimal viable product is that it can be — or is being — sold. Sometimes it's sold as an introductory or preview version (even if the purchase price is free), but there is something there that works.

As you start to decide when you will have a basic product, there are now a set of additional questions to answer. Basically, for most computer science projects, you will be looking at a sequence of deliverables. (There may be early-stage deliverables on a project such as a project proposal, a slide presentation, and the like, but those are not yet something that runs.)

Depending on what you are building, you have a variety of options. Here is an overview of the options, but you can have many, many others. This just gives you an idea of the possibilities for delivering your work.

You can plan on versions of an app or database (or any other computer science project). Typically, these versions are numbered 1, 2, 3... Intermediate versions can be numbered. It is not uncommon for a first release to be Version 1. It may quickly be followed by Version 1.1, which might contain some fixes for typos and other problems. You may continue on until Version 1 is stable. At that point, it's time to start thinking about Version 2.

As you move along, you can start to create a road map so that you have a sense of what your versions will be. This road map and schedule will turn into your project management tool. Typically the main versions (1, 2, 3) and perhaps major subdivisions (1.1, 2.3, etc.) are tied to marketing efforts (if they are apply). These milestones may also be tied to an academic calendar, milestones for funding (grant or investment), or other dates. Remember that once a milestone is attached to a date such as an academic calendar or a payment, it is no longer totally under the control of the computer science staff.

There's another aspect to When for you to consider. Once the project is stable, will it be used on a regular basis? If you are building a database to be maintained with products that will be popular around the year-end holidays, your critical time span for updating the database might be July (a typical lead time for year-end holiday data preparation). Plan what will be happening to and with your app, database, or other project.

Where Will the Project Run?

Although software may be imaginary, it needs devices on which to run. You have two major decisions about where you work will run. If it involves data that must be stored in a centralized location, the common practice is to host it on a web server; apps and websites can access it using the common REST protocol. There is typically a cost for that storage, but it can usually be managed fairly reasonable. Of course, if your project is for an organization that already has web storage available (a corporation, university, or private business), you may not have to worry.

Cloud platforms such as Amazon Web Services, Azure, and IBM let you use and easily configure cloud storage. These platforms are designed to react quickly to increased usage as a client suddenly needs more (or less) storage.

If you are building an app, you need to decide which platform it will run on. At the moment, there are four major mobile platforms:

- iOS

- Android

- Windows

- Web

Some apps must run on all of those platforms (think of an online banking app). Others can run on just one of them. In many cases, one platform is picked to start with. (Sort of a variation on minimal viable product.) Once it is running, it is possible to get feedback and, if necessary, additional support for further work on the project.

Microsoft has a Xamarin product that interests many people. It is based on .NET and C#. The goal is the elusive write once/run anywhere dream so that you can write code for iOS, Android, Windows, or macOS and have it run anywhere. The challenge with these strategies is that as modifications are made to the target systems, the combined system (like Xamarin) tends to lag behind. For many, many purposes, this is a very useful way of working. For others, the lack of contemporaneous support for the latest native OS features is a serious problem.

Regardless of your opinion, if you want to be a guide through the world of computer science to colleagues and clients, you need to understand the cross-platform and multi-platform issues.

How Will You Know the Results?

If you've decided what you're doing, who you're doing it for, why you're doing it, as well as when and where it will be used, you almost have the project plan for a computer science project mapped out. All that remains is to determine how to measure the status and success of the project.

Interestingly enough, this question that seems so obvious to many people is just as difficult for people to answer as the first one (what are you doing?). Once again, this is a question that didn't really matter too much in the non-digital world where you could see the results of your labors. You can measure sales or downloads of apps, but is that what you want? If you're working on an app that is designed to increase sales at a brick-and-mortar store, the downloads of the app don't matter nearly as much as the sales in the stores. If you are building a database of holiday gifts, the most obvious metric is the sales of those gifts. The web is littered with abandoned shopping carts on e-commerce sites (an oft-cited statistic is around 67% of shopping carts are abandoned, but that is from 2014 and online shopping sites are trying to bring that number down with new interface tools).

A major benefit of online app distribution such as the App Store is the wealth of data that is generated. (You can find a great deal of it on App Annie — `https://www.appannie.com.`) Many people find all those data incredibly useful, but if you really want to use it well, look at the data that will be available to you in the App Store and other metrics like App Annie and visitors to websites and databases. Look at what will be available and plan your results strategy. Don't wait until you have the data to decide what to do with it: set up your analysis right from the start.

That way, you can track your results.

Summary

This chapter shows you how computer science can fit into projects that you work on in other disciplines. As the world of apps takes shape (remember the App Store opened only in July 2008, less than 10 years before this book is being written), it is expected that people who know computer science know both the technology and the ways in which it can be used.

CHAPTER 14

Graphics and Visualization Techniques and Problems

You have seen examples of code, Xcode, and a storyboard in Chapters 11 and 12. In those cases as well as in the Swift playgrounds in other chapters, you can see code and principles of design and implementation. This chapter is different in that it does not focus on how to do one thing. Rather, this chapter walks through a real-life sequence of implementation questions and solutions. You can see how an interface evolves and how to look at it not as just a pretty picture but as something that is useful in conveying information and helping people work with an app that becomes useful to them.

© Jesse Feiler 2018
J. Feiler, *Learn Computer Science with Swift*, https://doi.org/10.1007/978-1-4842-3066-4_14

Introducing Utility Smart

The case study in this chapter is real. It traces the evolution of the interface of Utility Smart, an app designed to help people develop awareness of the natural resources that they use and to moderate their use of those resources.

The app starts from a simple idea: pose questions about recent use of resources to people and let them answer using sliders. There is background information that people can browse for more information, but the heart of the app is the sliders.

The data is saved on the device, and it can be plotted on a graph. The data is sharable using various technologies such as email and AirDrop. It was built for Swift and Cocoa Touch by Jesse Feiler. The Utility Smart project is led by Professor Curt Gervich of the Center for Earth and Environmental Science at State University of New York College at Plattsburgh. (If you want to see it in action, it is a free download from the App Store at `http://bit.ly/UtilitySmart`.)

Beginning the App (Utility Smart 1)

Using the basic questions from Chapter 13, we began by thinking about what we wanted to do. The point of the sliders was to provide a simple interface to let people enter their observed and behavioral data in less than a minute. Figure 14-1 shows the first iteration of the app. (Note that this is Version 1.0 of Utility Smart; it is no longer available in the App Store because it has been replaced with the later versions shown in this chapter.)

Figure 14-1. Sliders, version 1

To provide for flexibility, note that the interface uses a navigation controller and navigation item that provides the bar at the top of the window with Share button (left), and Save button (right). It is embedded in a tab bar controller (note the tabs at the bottom).

Note   The navigation controller provides the bar at the top of the window; the navigation item, which is the lower part of the navigation controller, is where the buttons and title are located.

This type of user interface is flexible because it's easy to add up to five tabs at the bottom, and, with the addition of more buttons in the navigation controller at the top, you easily have a variety of destinations from any view in the app.

Utility Smart has run on all iOS devices including iPad from the beginning, but many developers find it easier to work from the small devices and scale up than the reverse. That is the case here: the basic development is done on iPhone; Auto Layout is used for refinements.

The sliders are a useful part of the Cocoa Touch framework, and it's not difficult to reinforce the meaning of the settings by adjusting the background color to reflect the value of the slider. The code is shown later in this chapter, and the result is shown in Figure 14-2.

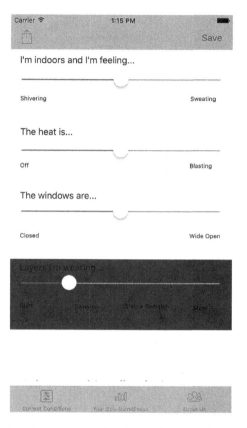

Figure 14-2. *Set background color based on slider value*

The interface you see in Figure 14-2 is quite impressive to demonstrate: you slide the slider back and forth and the background color changes (from red to green to red) to reflect the environmental impact. It's very impressive.

And not very subtle. Although we are working with small devices, their screens are powerful and, with today's resolutions, you don't need such blunt tools to get peoples' attention. Figure 14-3 shows the next iteration. It actually uses the same code based on the slider values; this time, instead of changing the background color of the slider view, the background color of the text is changed. In addition, the navigation bar's color is changed to a standard color for all of the app screens.

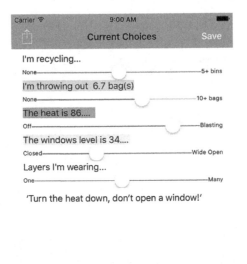

Figure 14-3. *Text backgrounds change*

There is space on the view for comments to be shown to encourage positive behaviors. (This is in addition to the colors of the text background.)

As you work with interfaces, you'll soon learn the cardinal rule: there is never enough space. (If you are designing a sign for the Goodyear blimp, there's not enough space.)

Figure 14-4 shows the introductory screen of Utility Smart 1.0 with scrolling text that extends beyond the window. In addition to not having enough room for all the text, project team discussions brought up the fact that there really should be two types of information:

- Information about the resource as shown in Figure 14-4 is one type of information.

- A second type of information — tips or advice — can help people learn what they can do to help use resources wisely.

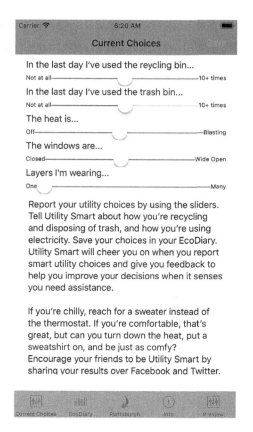

Figure 14-4. *Not enough space...*

It would be nice to have more space and to be able to differentiate between the two types of information. By emphasizing the different types of information in this and other cases, you can make it more usable for the user.

Refining the App (Utility Smart 2)

It's very common that as an app like this evolves, you have to stop complaining about not having enough space and do something about it. The solution for Utility Smart 2 is to break one aspect of the interface. Instead of putting all the sliders on one screen, if you split them apart with one slider per screen, you have much more space to work with. You lose the ability to see everything all at once, but you can have more space for information.

That is the approach taken in Utility Smart 2. Figure 14-5 shows a single slider.

Figure 14-5. *One slider per page*

There's much more space now for background information. Because the sliders are no longer on one screen, it doesn't make too much sense to share one slider's data, so that frees up the space at the left of the navigation item. It can be replaced with an Info button as you see in Figure 14-5. That button can be connected in the storyboard to a popover for a tip as you see in Figure 14-6.

Figure 14-6. *Tip popover*

This is a much more efficient use of space. It's more elegant and it is much more extensible for more information. Because popover views are full-fledged views, if you wanted to come back and put a video into a tip popover, that's easy to do.

One of the important lessons to learn in computer science is to constantly remember how you can implement features that have room for extension and expansion.

Another vital lesson to learn is that you can't design a good interface sitting at your desk. In fact, as a developer, you probably know too much about what the app can do to be able to build a useful interface for people who have never seen it before (or for people who have seen it before but approach it from a different perspective).

Figure 14-7 shows Utility Smart team members Curt Gervich, Maeve Sherry, and Michael Otton sharing interface ideas and reactions with a science class at Plattsburgh High School taught by Sonal Patel-Dame. Trying out ideas and suggestions with a broad range of users and potential users can help you refine your interface.

Figure 14-7.   *Utility Smart 2 interface brainstorming session*

Code Snippets

The code to implement parts of this interface is simple because it uses some very basic Cocoa Touch tools.

Creating a Popover: Code

The popover will be presented from a view controller. As is usually the case, you create a subclass of UIViewController. The important code is shown in Listing 14-1.

Here are the steps to implement the popover in the view controller:

- Make the view controller a UIPopoverPresentationControllerDelegate in the class declaration.

- Create the popover in the storyboard (shown in the following section).

- Implement prepare(for segue:) for the popover.

- Add adaptivePresentationStyle (for controller:) to manage popover size.

Listing 14-1. Creating a popover

```
import UIKit

class NowPageViewController: UIViewController,
UIPopoverPresentationControllerDelegate {

  ... code omitted

  override func prepare(for segue: UIStoryboardSegue,
  sender: Any?) {
    switch segue.identifier! {
    case "tipPopoverSegue":
      segue.destination.popoverPresentationController!
      .delegate = self
    default: break
    }
  }
}
```

```
func adaptivePresentationStyle(for controller:
UIPresentationController, traitCollection: UITraitCollection)
-> UIModalPresentationStyle
{
  return .none
}
```

... code omitted

Creating a Popover: Storyboard

In your storyboard, add a new view controller as you see in Figure 14-8. In
Figure 14-8 it has a title (label) and a text view. Select it and choose the Size
inspector in the utilities are. Set it to Freeform. Dimensions of 300x400 are
a good starting place for a popover.

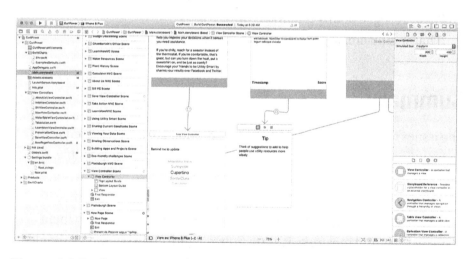

Figure 14-8. *Set popover size*

Control-drag from the view controller to the popover to create a segue.
Next, highlight the segue you have created as shown in Figure 14-9.

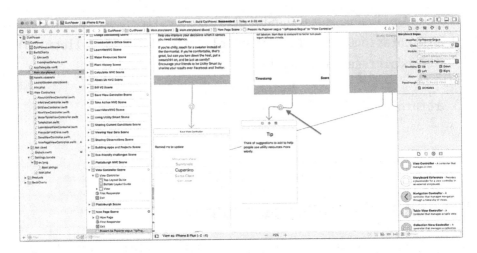

Figure 14-9. *Provide a name for the segue*

With the segue highlighted, click the Attributes inspector and name it. The name must match the name in `prepareForSegue` code — `tipPopoverSegue` in this example.

That should create the popover for you.

Summary

The issues of visualization and interface creation are best resolved with an iterative process and with input from as many people as possible. One caution: don't ask for interface advice directly, because people will give you answers based on other things they have seen. Watch what they do and try to do. See what confuses them. If you talk to them, talk to them about actions and meaning: it's your job to figure out what things should look like.

Index

D, E, F

G, H

Get the eBook for only $5!

Why limit yourself?

With most of our titles available in both PDF and ePUB format, you can access your content wherever and however you wish—on your PC, phone, tablet, or reader.

Since you've purchased this print book, we are happy to offer you the eBook for just $5.

To learn more, go to http://www.apress.com/companion or contact support@apress.com.

Apress®

Printed in the United States
By Bookmasters